# Teaching Language and Promoting Citizenship

## Edinburgh Textbooks in Applied Linguistics

Titles in the series include:

*An Introduction to Applied Linguistics*
*From Practice to Theory*
by Alan Davies

*Teaching Literature in a Second Language*
by Brian Parkinson and Helen Reid Thomas

*Materials Evaluation and Design for Language Teaching*
by Ian McGrath

*The Social Turn in Second Language Acquisition*
by David Block

*Language Assessment and Programme Evaluation*
by Brian Lynch

*Linguistics and the Language of Translation*
by Kirsten Malmkjaer

*Pragmatic Stylistics*
by Elizabeth Black

*Language Planning and Education*
by Gibson Ferguson

*Language and Politics*
by John E. Joseph

*Classroom Discourse and Teacher Development*
by Steve Walsh

*Materials Evaluation and Design for Language Teaching (2nd edition)*
by Ian McGrath

*Teaching Language and Promoting Citizenship*
by Mairin Hennebry-Leung and Angela Gayton

Visit the Edinburgh Textbooks in Applied Linguistics website at
www.euppublishing.com/series/eual

# Teaching Language and Promoting Citizenship

Mairin Hennebry-Leung and
Angela Gayton

EDINBURGH
University Press

For Sylvia and Mary.

'*We men and women are all in the same boat, upon a stormy sea. We owe to each other a terrible and tragic loyalty.*'
G. K. Chesterton, 1908

Edinburgh University Press is one of the leading university presses in the UK. We publish academic books and journals in our selected subject areas across the humanities and social sciences, combining cutting-edge scholarship with high editorial and production values to produce academic works of lasting importance. For more information visit our website: edinburghuniversitypress.com



Edinburgh University Press Ltd
The Tun – Holyrood Road, 12(2f) Jackson's Entry, Edinburgh EH8 8PJ

Typeset in 10/12 Adobe Garamond by
Servis Filmsetting Ltd, Stockport, Cheshire
and printed and bound in Great Britain.

A CIP record for this book is available from the British Library

ISBN 978 1 4744 2429 5 (hardback)
ISBN 978 1 4744 2431 8 (webready PDF)
ISBN 978 1 4744 2430 1 (paperback)
ISBN 978 1 4744 2432 5 (epub)

# Contents

# Series Editors' Preface

This series of single-author volumes published by Edinburgh University Press takes a contemporary view of applied linguistics. The intention is to make provision for the wide range of interests in contemporary applied linguistics which are provided for at the Master's level.

The expansion of Masters' postgraduate courses in recent years has had two effects:

1. What began almost half a century ago as a wholly cross-disciplinary subject has found a measure of coherence so that now most training courses in Applied Linguistics have similar core content.
2. At the same time the range of specialisms has grown, as in any developing discipline. Training courses (and professional needs) vary in the extent to which these specialisms are included and taught.

Some volumes in the series will address the first development noted above, while the others will explore the second. It is hoped that the series as a whole will provide students beginning postgraduate courses in Applied Linguistics, as well as language teachers and other professionals wishing to become acquainted with the subject, with a sufficient introduction for them to develop their own thinking in applied linguistics and to build further into specialist areas of their own choosing.

The view taken of applied linguistics in the Edinburgh Textbooks in Applied Linguistics Series is that of a theorising approach to practical experience in the language professions, notably, but not exclusively, those concerned with language learning and teaching. It is concerned with the problems, the processes, the mechanisms and the purposes of language in use.

Like any other applied discipline, applied linguistics draws on theories from related disciplines with which it explores the professional experience of its practitioners and which in turn are themselves illuminated by that experience. This two-way relationship between theory and practice is what we mean by a theorising discipline.

The volumes in the series are all premised on this view of applied linguistics as a theorising discipline which is developing its own coherence. At the same time, in order to present as complete a contemporary view of applied linguistics as possible other approaches will be expressed occasionally.

Each volume presents its author's own view of the state of the art in his or her topic. Volumes will be similar in length and in format, and, as is usual in a textbook series, each will contain exercise material for use in class or in private study.

Alan Davies
W. Keith Mitchell

# Introduction

Emerging global contexts have resurrected debates surrounding the concept of citizenship. In particular, vast increases in the numbers of refugees, asylum seekers and immigrants seeking to settle in new countries raise important questions, such as, what does it mean to be a *citizen* today? What kind of citizen might one aspire to become? Who is entitled to citizenship? What is the role of the state in promoting forms of citizenship that contribute to the flourishing of that particular society? What are the attributes needed by today's citizens for participating effectively in social and democratic processes and for pursuing personal fulfilment in our times?

## THE DEVELOPMENT OF CITIZENSHIP

Any discussion related to the understanding of citizenship takes us necessarily to the Greek and Roman origins of this concept. As Gorman (1992) argues in his detailed account of the Greek and Roman origins of citizenship, it is through comprehending the past that we can better understand our present. The notion of citizenship can be traced back to Athens and Sparta between the period from the sixth to the fourth centuries BC. At that time, being a citizen meant being willing to actively engage in public duties within the city, or the *polis*. The notion of citizenship in ancient Greece focused on a shared commitment to civic duties in matters of government and affairs of the state (Faulks, 2000). This civic republican view of citizenship required loyalty and active engagement from citizens who were expected to live according to shared values and rules. Entitlement to citizenship in ancient Greece was exclusively a male domain. Furthermore, family slaves were not entitled to citizenship. Even men could only become citizens by degrees, first through family membership as younger boys, later through a phratry,[1] then a tribe and finally at around eighteen years of age to the city.

Citizenship in the Roman Empire evolved to become more inclusive than in ancient Greece. Women, for instance, had the right to own property, engage in business or obtain a divorce. Certain rights of trade, marriage and migration were also conferred on the Latins, who had not been incorporated into the Roman Republic, or to certain Roman colonies. Slaves in the Roman Empire lacked legal personhood and were considered personal property instead. Nevertheless, over time they acquired certain protections under Roman law and could even attain citizenship when manumitted. Much as in ancient Greece, male Roman citizens enjoyed the widest range of privileges and protections. A citizen could, under certain exceptional circumstances, be deprived of his citizenship. Significantly, Roman legal systems enshrined the principle that individuals could become citizens by law rather than birth, thus making citizenship accessible to a wider population and recognising as paramount the relationship between the individual and the state. Another important feature of citizenship in the Roman Empire, was the possibility for children of former slaves who had gained their freedom to become citizens themselves. In the Roman Empire we see the roots of citizenship markers that are seen in many contexts of today's world, such as ancestry, birthplace and loyalty to the state.

In its earlier modern forms, the concept of citizenship developed in response to authority, whether papal, dynastic or monarchic, as is seen in early theorising on citizenship for instance by John Locke, Jean-Jacques Rousseau, Immanuel Kant and Georg Wilhelm Friedrich Hegel. In these theorisations citizenship has been closely connected to specific historical power struggles, political contexts and diverse stages of national development. Ruffer (2012) argues that the political theory on citizenship that has emerged from the seventeenth-century birth of the Westphalian European state system, through the Enlightenment period of the eighteenth century and into the present day, has considered as central to democratic conceptualisations of citizenship (p. 189) the value of individual rights, equality, liberty, expression of universal moral imperative and, in recent times, the reformulation of the meaning of communication and diversity, among others.

The notion of the individual as a free and morally responsible political agent has been defended through revolutions and proclamations of independence, such as the French Declaration of the Rights of Man and of the Citizen and the US Declaration of Independence and their many derivations, as basic tenets inserted in the constitution of different countries.

During the late nineteenth-century and early twentieth-century Industrial Revolution, citizen rights were expanded beyond propertied white males and citizenship began to be more strongly associated with state, territory and rights. The enshrinement of citizenship in law was prompted in part by the need of emerging industrial democracies of the time to better define and secure national borders and deal with new colonial territories and increased migration. Thus, citizenship entitlement was based on territorial or birthright (*jus soli*), descent (*jus sanguinis*) or a combination of the two. In a range of countries, birthplace and ancestry continue to be perceived as key markers of citizenship entitlement (McCrone and Bechhofer 2008). In this sense, while national identity has often been seen as fluid, complex and contextual (Brubaker and Cooper 2000), citizenship has traditionally been viewed more rigidly, as a label rather than peformance. Yet, as we will see through the course of this book, emerging notions show an increasing tendency towards conceptualisations of citizenship as a resource that people *use* or something that they *do*, fulfilling certain conditions, rather than attributes they *have* or *are* (Jamieson 2002).

In 1948 the Universal Declaration of Human Rights (UDHR) conceived citizenship as the right to membership in one's sovereign nation, closely tying citizenship to a territory and a national people, and guaranteeing certain civil rights. Thus, the Declaration sought, in a way, to guarantee state citizenship to all individuals. By encompassing the state system within the international human rights order, through international treaties and institutional structures such as the International Court of Justice and the European Court of Human Rights, individuals were extended the guarantee of individual human rights and protection against statelessness.

The economic expansion and increased flow of labour migration since World War II, resulted in a growing number of non-citizens as long-term or permanent residents in Western liberal democracies. In both cases, non-citizens possessed full access to liberal civil and social rights. This ongoing situation created a need to reconsider understandings of citizenship and generated discussion particularly around the notion of social cohesion, as largely monocultural societies rapidly transformed into multicultural ones. Some scholars connected the growing percentage of 'foreign' populations in Western liberal democracies with a 'devaluation' of the concept of citizenship, while others focused on developing a concept of multicultural citizenship fit for liberal democracy.

The late twentieth century saw the collapse of Eastern European communism and the fragmentation of national borders into smaller ethnic units. At this time also, the international system of human rights was further developed to provide a legal structure for the acquisition of rights beyond national borders. Some scholars interpreted these events as signalling the end of the Westphalian system of national states and the birth of post-national citizenship, while others proposed notions of multiple citizenship, wherein the national state constituted the primary political form of membership and sovereign authority. Indeed, we can talk about ideas of the national citizen, the European citizen, the global citizen, the cosmopolitan citizen, and so on. In other words, today's citizen operates within and across multiple spheres and domains requiring the skills to communicate and act in ways that are contextually appropriate to each one, while enabling the individual to effectively take hold of and exercise their rights, and their social and moral responsibilities.

## CITIZENSHIP AND IDENTITY

Citizenship can be viewed as an external, legally defined marker of an internal identity. Yet, this internal identity is also shaped by the actions and reactions generated by the external marker. Kiely et al. (2001) propose national identity markers to be 'those social characteristics presented to others to support a national identity claim and looked for in others, either to attribute national identity, or receive and assess any claims or attributions made' (pp. 35–36). To a certain extent, this can be considered to be true also of citizenship. As a legal concept, in order to enable effective execution of the relationship between the state and the individual, citizenship needs to be clearly defined. However, at the social level, citizenship is a more fluid concept that overlaps with ideas of identity and group membership. Rapid expansion and unexpected exits from the European Union, the heightened global threat of terrorism and the ongoing refugee and displacement crisis being heralded as the greatest humanitarian and refugee crisis on record (UNHCR 2018) are significant examples of social phenomena that have fuelled heated debates around ideas of citizenship, inclusion and exclusion, and identity. Indeed, such phenomena have also given significant impetus to the introduction and development of citizenship education in contexts such as the United Kingdom, while contexts where citizenship education was already integrated into the curriculum have expressed continued commitment to such education and have seen this as an opportunity to reflect on existing content and pedagogy of these studies.

There has been some academic discussion regarding the distinction between citizenship and identity. Brettell (2011), for instance, distinguishes between political belonging and cultural belonging, extending this to a distinction between citizenship (reason) and identity (emotion). Binary distinctions on the basis of a reason/emotion dichotomy have too often been used to create a gender divide and to foment gender discrimination. As a result there has been decreasing acceptance of this position and increasing recognition that identity and citizenship are closely intertwined and can be difficult to tease apart within the individual's psyche. Pointing to the interwoven relationship between citizenship and identity, Brettell's (2011) participants saw citizenship as a combination of civic rights/responsibilities and civic identity. In this sense both aspects respond to socio- and geo-political contexts and are co-constructed, combining the way one is perceived and the way one perceives oneself. The citizenship conferred on an individual is one marker of how others perceive them and so can be said to be one factor in shaping identity, though what factors are involved in determining the conferral of citizenship is clearer from a legal perspective than from a social one. National inclusion has traditionally been determined through conferring citizenship to those fulfilling requirements of residency within national borders (Stewart 2000). In this case, conferment of citizenship operates as a mechanism of external and internal territorial exclusion. Thus, citizenship is used to signal group membership, in itself a marker of identity. Indeed, Gilbertson and Singer (2003) propose that traditional conceptualisations of citizenship are being challenged by the emergence of what they term transnational citizenship. This is supported by other scholars who argue that the idea of 'the citizen who spent most of his life or her life in one country and shared a common national identity is losing ground' (Castles 2004: 18).

The notion that identity and citizenship are intertwined also plays an important part in Heater's (1990) model of citizenship, which has informed much of the philosophy behind this volume. The model proposes five key elements that comprise citizenship: identity, virtue, legal/civil, political and social. The deep need human beings have to belong to a community is well-researched and -established, but Heater goes further to suggest that the individual who 'has no sense of civic bond with his fellows or of some responsibility for civic welfare is not a true citizen' (p. 182). Citizenship is seen by Heater as one form of identity, both because through exercising citizenship individuals develop moral maturity, growing as a social being, and because, in his view, citizenship overlays other expressions of social identity. He argues that, while other social identities, e.g. religious, ethnic, sexual, class, can be the source of intense emotion and antagonism, being a citizen is somehow different. Indeed, citizenship, at least in its essence promotes egalitarian and all-embracing principles. Of course, as Heater acknowledges, the enactment of citizenship and the debates around citizenship entitlement may suggest a different reality; nonetheless the accepted model of citizenship bears an egalitarian potential.

## LIBERAL AND REPUBLICAN CONCEPTS OF CITIZENSHIP

While conceptualisations of citizenship depend to a large degree on the philosophical starting point, it is possible to broadly conceive two approaches to the concept, one a *liberal* stance and the other a *civic republican/communitarian* approach (Dwyer 2010). There have historically been two main ideas of civil liberties and of the kinds of citizenship associated with each: a *liberal* idea and a *republican* idea (Crick 2000). The former views civil liberties as a legal framework for protecting the individual against the state, while the latter is a positive means through which citizens can play a part in shaping and influencing society. The liberal stance stresses the importance of individually-held rights, while the republican emphasises the individual's commitment and obligations to the wider community (Heater 1999; Dwyer 2000). Faulks' (2000) discussion of citizenship suggests that the two notions are interrelated, making the idea of citizenship inherently appealing to those of varying political persuasions. On the one hand, citizenship rights offer the space for individuals to pursue their interests free from interferences, as well as the opportunity to participate in shaping common governmental institutions. Citizenship, therefore, is also an inherently relational concept entailing cooperation between individuals in the running of their lives. Thus, in addition to rights, the citizen also has duties and responsibilities. Being a citizen implies being included in the wider community. On the one hand it recognises the contribution the individual makes to the community, while on the other hand it grants them autonomy, as reflected in the rights conferred on the individual. In themselves these rights are an acknowledgement of the political agency of the individual.

## ACTIVE CITIZENSHIP

Citizenship not only offers benefits to the individual, but it is also a reciprocal and social idea. It can never be purely a set of rights that free the individual from obligations to others. Instead, where there are rights there must also be structures and mechanisms through which these rights are recognised and fulfilled. These frameworks, such as schools, courts, hospitals and parliaments, require all citizens to play their part. Thus, citizenship and citizens' rights imply duties and obligations also for the individual. It is not possible to have one without the other. Faulks (2000) goes so far as to argue that while it may be possible to imagine a society that functions justly without a formal expression of rights, it is more difficult to imagine a stable human community where there is not some sense of obligation between its members. Indeed, this echoes the sentiment expressed by Skinner (1986), 'unless we place our duties before our rights, we must expect to find our rights themselves undermined'. This notion of civic participation and obligation can be traced back to T. H. Marshall's (1950) seminal discussion of citizenship. Marshall (1950) viewed civil, political and social rights as central to citizenship theory. He went on, however, to propose that the status of citizen entails not only rights, but also duties and responsibilities. Lister (2003) took this notion forward and proposed that citizenship entails a relationship between citizenship as status and citizenship as practice. In this way, modern conceptualisations have come to embrace both the traditions named by these authors, one as liberal and the other as republican. The citizen is able to claim rights, but the existence of these rights also presupposes duties, obligations and participation in the structures, mechanisms and relationships that make these rights feasible. Heater (1990) describes the 'good citizen' as 'one who so orders his life that at least a part of it is consciously directed to the benefit of the society in which he lives (however defined)' (p. 332). A key distinguishing characteristic then of citizenship as opposed to subjecthood is an ethic of participation; citizenship is an active rather than a passive status. Citizenship is not simply conferred, it is also practised. Constructive participation in society depends also on a sense of belonging, or group membership.

Citizenship then can be said to be an interaction between rights, access, belonging and responsibilities. Citizenship is conferred on the individual but is also practised. The conferred status is an acknowledgement or external signal of assigned group membership, which is also strengthened through the active practice of citizenship. The external and internal reinforcing of group membership strengthens a sense of civic identity, which in turn promotes greater participation.

| Conferred Citizenship<br>*(Status)*<br>↓ • Rights<br>↓ • Access<br>↓ • Belonging<br>↓ • Responsibilities | ↔ Identity ↔ | Practised Citizenship<br>*(Active)*<br>• Rights ↑<br>• Access ↑<br>• Belonging ↑<br>• Responsibilities ↑ |
|---|---|---|

*Figure I.1* Interactive components of citizenship

Active citizenship is likely to mean different things in different social spheres or different socio-cultural contexts (Nelson and Kerr 2006). Yet some commonly agreed principles seem to emerge through the literature. Active citizens can be understood as those who construct civil society, who sustain social solidarity by exerting influence in public life, employing critical capacities to weigh evidence before speaking and acting (Blunkett and Taylor 2010; Crick and Lockyer 2010). Crick (2000) takes a rather disparaging tone when drawing a distinction between the active citizen and the *good* citizen and contrasting perceptions of citizenship in France and the United States with perceptions in Britain:

> In Britain, however, the qualifying adjective for citizen has less often been 'active' than 'good'. Good citizens have a respect for law and order, pay their taxes . . . know their place in society . . . keep their noses clean and are ever so grateful to be governed so well, although we British do rather pride ourselves (or used to) on knowing our rights . . . Only recently on environmental issues have neighbours begun to combine for political or 'community' action'. (p. 98)

The implication is, once again, that citizenship is not simply conferred and passively received, but must also be exercised as a means of supporting existing social structures and citizenship as actively constructing and shaping society. Ke and Starkey (2014) propose that civic participation involves citizens engaging in discussions relating to politics or public policies, while also implying community involvement. The *active* citizen, they suggest, is one who participates in society and community, while the *good* citizen seeks to 'obey the law, be polite and well-behaved, respect individual rights, address moral virtues of care and concern for others, be good neighbours etc.' (p. 52).

Nelson and Kerr (2006) surveyed active citizenship practices across fifteen countries and found that present understandings of active citizenship seem to converge on the following points:

> active citizenship . . .
> . . . is fundamentally about engagement and participation
> . . . focuses on participation in both civil and civic society
> . . . is increasingly framed in the context of lifelong and life wide learning
> . . . involves the active development of citizenship dimensions not just knowledge and understanding, but skills' development and behaviours picked up through experience of participation in a range of contexts
> . . . includes both 'active' and 'passive' elements
> . . . encompasses theoretical approaches to citizenship – liberal, communitarian and civic republican – and ranges from more conformist, collective actions and behaviours to those that are more individualistic and challenge driven. (p. iv)

There is a sense that across cultural contexts, citizenship is coming to be understood beyond a relationship between individual and state, and instead as a relationship between the participatory, agentive individual, their community and society. Furthermore, what is meant by community and society today has been considerably expanded by notions emanating from the concept of the *cosmopolitan citizen.*

## BEYOND NATIONAL CITIZENSHIP

The work of Audrey Osler and Hugh Starkey has been fundamental in proposing the notion of the *cosmopolitan citizen*. Their premise is that in today's global context, with the increased threat of terrorism, the emergence of new forms of racism, the reality of super-diversity and the increasing popularity of far-right political parties and populist movements, an educational focus on the arguments of national citizenship maybe be misguided or even a threat to cohesive society (Osler and Starkey 2018). Instead, they propose that what is needed is education for cosmopolitan citizenship (Osler and Vincent 2002; Osler and Starkey 2003), whereby young people are prepared and equipped for living in increasingly diverse societies with political efficacy and the opportunity for practising their citizenship. This idea is further explored in Chapter 1, but its core principles, reflecting also the notion of intercultural citizenship (Byram 2008), are central to the discussion of citizenship throughout this book, referring not simply to national citizenship but to the wider conceptualisation of citizenship required in today's global context.

Enactment of this active and cosmopolitan citizenship requires that citizens are adequately prepared to take up their role and, to this end, schools and education more broadly have been seen as a primary means of civic socialisation (Kamens 1988). Citizenship practice, in its fullest sense, requires an understanding of the rights and of the duties and obligations of such citizens. Furthermore, it demands an awareness of the mechanisms and processes through which to participate in and contribute to society and the forms that such participation and contribution might take. But, knowledge in itself is not enough, as Heater (1990) points out:

> one may be born a little citizen in status, but one must learn about the rights and duties, the attitudes and skills this status entails. Citizenship is meaningless if that learning does not take place; defective if the educational process is not thorough. (p. 319)

Indeed, he goes further to suggest that the citizen is by definition, 'a person furnished with knowledge of public affairs, instilled with attitudes of civic virtue and equipped with skills to participate in the political arena' (p. 336), which in a way may restrict *a contrario sensu* the concept of citizenship by devaluing participation in citizenship through the more egalitarian legal and emotional lines. This may happen if the title of 'citizen' were to be applied only to those who have the high education necessary for the conscious exercise of their rights and responsibilities. In other words, citizenship is not simply a conferment of rights, but the development of a mindset. There appears also to exist a responsibility by the state/nation to equip its citizens with skills and knowledge, in order to play a part in society:

> Knowledge about citizenship is only partially useful if it does not lead on to the formulation of attitudes and the acquisition of skills; attitudes are but prejudices unless grounded in a firm and clear understanding; and action is wanting direction without attitudes and is irresponsible and/or inefficient if born in ignorance'. (Heater 1990, pp. 336–337)

The notion of *active citizenship* has for some time been considered the goal towards which citizenship education initiatives should work (Ireland et al. 2006; Nelson and Kerr 2006). This focus has increased as traditional concepts of citizenship, defined in relation to government institutions, have been challenged. In addition to the unique phenomena outlined earlier, challenges emerging in the latter half of the twentieth century have also included growing recognition of the rights of minority groups and of indigenous people, the collapse of political structures, the emergence of new ones and the increasing global population (Kerr 1999: 12). Thus, the concept of active citizenship has been present in much of the recent discussion and debate around citizenship education. References to civic participation in policy documents, for instance from the Qualifications and Curriculum Authority (1999) or the House of Commons Education and Skills Committee (2007), bear witness to this. Furthermore, the practice of active cosmopolitan citizenship necessitates skills and attitudes that enable the individuals to decentre, to critically examine their own beliefs, values and assumptions as well as those of others, and to be able to find constructive ways to build intercultural bridges, both within their immediate community and beyond. This is true today in everyday interactions, in the forging of social relationships and in the workplace. Few curriculum areas would be better placed than language teaching to facilitate the offer to students of a close exposure to other ways of life, other forms of expression, other value frameworks, and for the opening up of opportunities for examining and reflecting on their own value framework, their own identities and their ability to see and create connections across cultural communities; since it is through language that we enact our identities, express our values and forge human relatedness:

> Language links its interlocutors in a dynamic, reflexive process. We learn about people through what they say and how they say it; we learn about ourselves through the ways that other people react to what we say; and we learn about our relationship with others through the give and take of communicative interactions. (Bonvillain, 2003: 1)

Byram (2001) emphatically declares that 'language teaching as foreign language education cannot and should not avoid educational and political duties and responsibilities' (p. 102), duties which he frames in promoting an education for intercultural citizenship in the foreign language classroom. Indeed the complementarity of language education, emphasising intercultural communicative competence, and citizenship education, emphasising civic action in the community, is well established in the literature (Byram 1997; Liddicoat and Scarino 2013; Porto, Houghton and Byram 2017). Language teaching is seen to have not only an instrumental purpose but perhaps more importantly an educational purpose, and it is here that the aims of language teaching and the aims of citizenship education converge (Byram et al. 2017).

> Language teaching for intercultural communication is front and center in the educational mission of facilitating our students' participation in intercultural citizenship, which is a sine qua non in today's world. (Byram and Wagner 2018: 149)

This introduction has thus advanced the conceptual framework for the discussion that aims to develop throughout the book. It has explored the notion of citizenship from its beginnings in classical civilisations to today, considering also the increased emphasis on active citizenship, and the accompanying shift towards models of participatory citizenship whereby rights lead also to responsibilities. Finally, the chapter has highlighted several of the consequences of increased social diversity, of the importance that these have in how citizenship is conceived and of the tools for its rich and full enactment.

## NOTE

1. In ancient Greece, a phratry was a defined social division. Enrolment in a phratry was a basic requirement for Greek citizenship.

Chapter 1

# Understanding citizenship from the national to the cosmopolitan

**Objectives**

- To understand key conceptualisations of citizenship.
- To critically engage with some of the challenges and opportunities presented by each conceptualisation.
- To understand the core principles at the heart of emerging cosmopolitan citizenship.
- To develop awareness of seminal works that have shaped current conceptualisations of citizenship.

## INTRODUCTION

This chapter outlines the complex ground between conceptualisations of citizenship at national and global levels, reflecting also on notions of citizenship that emerge at the regional level. This analysis paves the way for an examination of the challenges and opportunities that notions of citizenship present for the language teacher specifically and educationalists more generally. Diverse understandings of citizenship are shaped by the history, philosophy and culture of a people. The socio- and geo-political contexts in which a people lives and moves constitute a further important source of influence. This is clear when we compare national, regional and cosmopolitan citizenship, all of which operate within different interrelating spheres, with each sphere being characterised by distinct geo- and socio-political features.

## NATIONAL CITIZENSHIP

Marshall's (1950) seminal model of citizenship has been instrumental in shaping how we understand citizenship at the present time, while providing a framework for many of the educational approaches to citizenship in today's democratic societies. The model proposes a tripartite view of citizenship comprising three aspects: the civil, the political and the social. The civil refers to rights underpinning individual freedoms, such as freedom of speech, the right to justice and liberty of the person; the political refers to the right of participation in the exercise of political power, for instance through voting mechanisms; and the social comprises the freedom to reach full individual and social potential, also understood as the right to freely pursue happiness within the remit of the law and without violation of the rights of others, as enshrined for instance in the United States Declaration of Independence. The implementation and application of these elements vary according to the *bounded* or *unbounded* nature of citizenship in the given context (Noels, Yashima and Zhang 2011).

Bounded citizenship is legally defined and usually enacted within national borders. These borders have come as a result of economic, political and racial history. They are intended to mark membership of a given group as well as determining the legitimacy of claims to identity and rights. Questions about access to citizenship, both in terms of inclusion and exclusion, the rights that accompany citizenship and the relationship between the individual and the state, are all relevant in the context of bounded citizenship (Byrne 2014), but are less applicable to unbounded citizenship. Unbounded citizenship is not legally defined and is practised in a context free of borders; in other words its practice is not confined by any legal or geographic borders, as can be seen for instance in the case of cosmopolitan citizenship. The absence of a geographical or legal border is accompanied also by a lack of institutional frameworks through which citizenship is conferred. Consequently, within unbounded citizenship there is no relationship between the individual and the state because there is no state of which to speak. Instead the focus becomes the relationship between the individual and the society, arguably shifting the emphasis from the responsibility of the state to the individual to the responsibility of the citizen to the community or society they inhabit.

Bounded citizenship is typically enacted at the level of the nation state and in this context Marshall's three strands are most easily identifiable. Nation states confer on their citizens certain rights and responsibilities, for instance abiding by the governing laws of the society and holding and being held to account. Similarly, political institutions and mechanisms through which citizens participate in governance are clearly identifiable in bounded forms of citizenship, whether as election processes, non-governmental organisations or local communities. The social strand takes different forms at the national level depending on the individual's aspirations and the means through which they think they can best serve the community and the society. This strand is arguably the most transferable across bounded and unbounded forms of citizenship, while the civil and political strands become more complex in unbounded forms, where the establishment of global political and civil institutions and relevant participatory structures is, unavoidably, more unwieldy.

## REGIONAL CITIZENSHIP

Around the globe there are examples of unions between nation states, set up often for political reasons, but entailing also attempts at creating a regional sense of identity and a form of citizenship that sits between the unbounded and bounded realms. Examples include, for instance, the Organization of American States (OAS), the Association of Southeast Asian Nations (ASEAN), the League of Arab States (the Arab League) and even in some regards, the European Union. All four of these examples were established with the key aims of promoting regional stability as well as economic and political cooperation. Also integral to the stated goals are notions of collaboration around cultural, social and welfare matters. Such unions have comparable aims, acknowledging the sovereignty of individual nation states, while also looking to form ties beyond national borders to work towards a common goal.

In the case of ASEAN and the EU, attempts have been made to generate a sense of community identity, specifically through symbols such as a union flag, an emblem, a commemorative day and an anthem. Regional unions can offer spaces for exercising citizenship values beyond national borders, whether through the practices of individual citizens or through concerted cooperation between nation states.

Unlike ASEAN and the Arab League, the EU has more explicitly sought to establish and promote a distinct notion of citizenship associated with Union membership. This particular citizenship is contingent on national citizenship, but is enacted beyond national borders. Marshall's political, civil and social strands are evident in the form of citizenship the EU has sought to promote. The introduction of European citizenship to the European Community Treaty in 1992 conferred on European citizens certain civic rights such as the right to freedom of movement and residence and the right to diplomatic protection. The right to vote in European elections embodies Marshall's political strand, while the social strand is manifest through participatory initiatives such as educational exchanges and social enterprises.

Regional unions seeking to promote notions of an associate citizenship face a number of challenges. The first of these is that they walk a fine line, on the one hand facilitating community that goes beyond national confines, and arguably enabling greater inclusion, but on the other hand extending the boundaries of exclusion and an insider/outsider dichotomy. Indeed, in some sense it may be argued that the unity between states can serve to strengthen inclusion or exclusion policies, depending on the socio-political current of the time. The second challenge is in gathering sufficient popular support to legitimise the notion. The challenge of uniting a citizenry around shared values and aspirations is already considerable at the national level and becomes all the more complex at the regional level, where particular visions may be agreed on by governments but are not necessarily easily adopted by the demos.

## COSMOPOLITAN CITIZENSHIP

Beyond national and institutional settings and regional unions, cosmopolitan citizenship takes a more unbounded form. Within cosmopolitan citizenship, actualisation of the three citizenship strands, particularly the civil and political, becomes more complex given the lack of institutional loci for the citizen. Moreover, the fact that decision-making at a global level is invariably undertaken by unelected non-governmental institutions poses challenges for establishing processes of democratisation and for the creation of participatory structures for the exercise of the citizens' rights and responsibilities. The space within which cosmopolitan citizenship is enacted is not under the jurisdiction of any one state and thus decision-making in this context requires complex processes of negotiation and mediation. Nevertheless, Osler and Starkey (2003) argue that the concept of cosmopolitan citizenship is useful for understanding and conceptualising the emergence of 'trans-national and diasporic communities composed of individuals entitled to and aware of their human rights' (p. 246). Drawing on the UNESCO framework (1995), they propose that educated cosmopolitan citizens will

> work to achieve peace, human rights and democracy within the local community and at a global level, by:
>
> - accepting personal responsibility and recognising the importance of civic commitment;
> - working collaboratively to solve problems and achieve a just, peaceful and democratic community;
> - respecting diversity between people, according to gender, ethnicity and culture;
> - recognising that their own worldview is shaped by personal and societal history and by cultural tradition;
> - respecting the cultural heritage and protecting the environment;
> - promoting solidarity and equity at national and international levels. (pp. 246–247)

When understood in this way we can begin to perceive common ground between the various forms of citizenship we have discussed. The values highlighted in this conceptualisation of cosmopolitan citizenship reflect also those in the European Commission's conceptualisation and promotion of European citizenship, which outlines a commitment to:

- contributing to citizens' understanding of the EU, its history and diversity.
- fostering European citizenship and improve conditions for civic and democratic participation at EU level.
- raising awareness of remembrance, the common history and values of the EU and the EU's aim – namely to promote peace, the values of the EU and the well-being of its peoples.
- encouraging the democratic and civic participation of citizens at EU level. (European Commission 2016)

Meanwhile, those seeking, for instance, British citizenship are required to uphold similar values such as 'individual liberty', 'tolerance of those with different faiths and beliefs' and 'participation in community life' (Great British Home Office 2013). Thus, across bounded and unbounded citizenship it is possible to identify core values intended to enhance social cohesion and a respect for diversity and individual freedoms. This common ground is essential in developing an education for citizenship that offers the opportunity to reflect on the role of the individual both within and beyond the national confines, acknowledging the human connection that goes beyond geo-political borders and ties the individual to one's fellow man by virtue of the values one holds rather than the geography of where one was born. The values that are shared across the spheres of citizenship seen here constitute a useful basis on which the teacher can encourage learners to appreciate diversity and to seek to play a part in society in all its forms and spheres.

Active and participatory citizenship at every level presupposes shared values and understandings such that individuals are able to work towards a common vision of society. This cannot be taken for granted in culturally diverse and even divergent contexts where assumptions about the nature of humanity and society and the values that are to be respected may vary across cultural groups. Thus, while such diversity can lead to an enrichment of society and a deepened intra- and interpersonal understanding, it needs critical and explicit exploration for the purposes of agreeing on a shared set of values and a common framework within which it would be appreciated and upheld. Enabling individuals to find ways for constructive collaboration, where arriving at a framework of shared values may be impossible, is also a must. It is particularly within these two situations where education, and language education specifically, can play a key part if prepared to do so.

## CITIZENSHIP AND EDUCATION

Building on the work of Marshall, Stewart (1995) and Wiener (1996) propose that a full conceptualisation of citizenship must entail *rights*, *access* and *belonging*; providing a possible framework for the role that education may play in promoting citizenship. While, as we have seen, *rights* can be interpreted differently across bounded and unbounded forms of citizenship, the principles still apply. There are rights that pertain to each sphere of citizenship, whether in terms of civic rights or human rights. Similarly, participatory citizenship in all spheres will be contingent on a sense of *belonging*. It is in the realm of *access* and *belonging* that education arguably plays the most important role, on the one hand making learners aware of their membership in society at the local, national, supra-national and global levels, on the other hand providing the tools with which to fully enact this membership. These tools enable *access*, the degree to which citizens are able actually to take hold of and exercise the rights and responsibilities conferred on them. Simply conferring these rights is not enough; there must be mechanisms and structures in place to enable the exercise of these same rights. Starkey (2005) further suggests that in order to exercise their rights, citizens 'must be familiar with them and understand the scope and the limitations of their rights' (p. 25). Indeed this might be extended from rights to responsibilities also. In the spirit of active participatory citizenship, individuals need to be aware of the processes through which they can enact their citizenship and contribute meaningfully to society whether at a local or global level.

The final report of the Advisory Group on Citizenship, commonly referred to as the Crick Report, stated: 'Civic spirit, citizens' charters and voluntary activity in the community are of crucial importance, but individuals must be helped and prepared to shape the terms of such engagements by political understanding and action' (Advisory Group on the Teaching of Citizenship and Democracy in Schools

1998: 10). The Advisory Group suggested that all citizens, primarily through the means of education, should be equipped with the political skills needed to shape laws in a peaceful and responsible manner, in other words playing an active part in shaping society. Furthermore, the Group went on to argue that volunteering and community involvement are necessary conditions of a civil society in a democracy as a means of promoting the sense of belonging intrinsic to current conceptualisations of democratic citizenship. The Crick Report maintains that while voluntary and community activity do not capture the full meaning of active citizenship, freedom and full citizenship in the political arena nevertheless depend on a society with a rich variety of non-political associations and voluntary groups as a basis. This contention is supported by findings of a comparative survey of Britain and the United States conducted by Crewe, Searing and Conover (1997), which pointed to a consistently strong association between electoral turnout, attention to political and public issues in the media, involvement in election campaigns and demonstrations on the one hand and motivations reinforced through participation in informal groups and voluntary associations on the other.

Throughout the report, the Advisory Group on Citizenship insisted that preparation for active participatory citizenship should be an explicit part of education. Indeed, this argument is widely and consistently promoted and supported in the relevant literature. Education is considered the primary means of socialisation (Kamens 1988), thus playing a key role in the promotion and preservation of citizenship and identity. The Crick Report supported this idea by placing heavy emphasis on the role of formal education in developing active citizens, namely citizens who would seek out opportunities for democratic involvement for the common good.

Civic engagement can be understood and expressed in a variety of different ways. As a psychological concept, it can be defined in terms of a sense of efficacy, political cognition and levels of interest in politics (Verba, Schlozman and Brady 1995). As Whiteley explains, such a view results in the goal of education being that of 'increasing political knowledge, promoting citizenship interest in politics and public affairs and reinforcing the individual's sense of efficacy' (2005: 4).

A second approach to civic engagement is in sociological terms accounting for 'people's connections with the life of their communities, not merely with politics' (Putnam 1995: 665). Whiteley argues that through this interpretation, 'education helps to build and develop social capital, or network actors who are civically engaged within their communities' (2005: 4).

A further possible approach views civic engagement as tiers of creating autonomous, rational individuals capable of identifying and pursuing their own political interests and articulating these in the public realm (Nie, Junn and Stehlik-Barry 1996).

In synthesis, in these different understandings of civic engagement, two key elements of citizenship emerge as: (a) participation through volunteering and community involvement; (b) participation through political understanding and action. Together (a) and (b) appear to tie in the civic, political and social strands of citizenship of Marshall's (1950) model through a habitual interaction, but their enactment is underpinned by the concepts of *rights*, *access* and *belonging*. Indeed this has been recognised extensively in policy statements at every level of extraction. A submission from the Citizenship Foundation in response to the UK government's 1997 White Paper, *Excellence in Schools*, states that:

> citizenship has a clear conceptual core which relates to the induction of young people into the legal, moral and political arena of public life. It introduces pupils to society and its constituent elements, and shows how they, as individuals, relate to the whole. (As cited in Crick 2000)

Such a statement paves the way for education to play a part in the promotion of citizenship within every sphere, given that human society's learners inhabit today's world beyond any local or indeed national context; even where learners do not physically cross borders to encounter other cultures and countries, those cultures and countries are brought to them through the multicultural nature of societies today. Indeed '*public life*' without multicultural dialogue and interactions is today scarcely conceivable, and so education for citizenship seeks to develop individuals able to transition effectively across contexts while contributing meaningfully to society in its various guises.

While the role of schools varies across contexts, these educational establishments can be argued to be in a unique position to provide exposure to the world that exists beyond their students' immediacy; and, importantly, they can generate opportunities for critical and guided consideration of the individual's role within that world (Taylor 1993). Taylor suggests that two school subjects have traditionally addressed the wider world, namely history and geography. He states:

> Schools are agents of human resource development and societal change. Pupils need opportunities to develop their talents and inform their judgments in order to participate constructively across ethnic and national frontiers. The morality underpinning this participation will be partly formed in the school. (1993: 442)

As Taylor points out, the increasing opportunities available to travel, live and work freely across national contexts will prove advantageous to those who are given the education to benefit from such mobility and in turn contribute to its development. Taylor was writing in the context of the European Community and with reference to the right to freedom of movement conferred on European citizens. However, the principle should be applied with similar weight within the context of any citizenship sphere. Indeed, his argument goes beyond the instrumental considerations of employment, highlighting the significance of a *morality* that underpins civic participation within and beyond frontiers and that is common to both national and cosmopolitan citizenship.

It is interesting to note that the notion of morality is intrinsically intertwined with conceptualisations of citizenship, as is evidenced in Kennedy, Fairbrother and Zhenxhou's (2014) edited volume, where the terms *citizenship education*, *civic education* and *moral education* are used interchangeably. In the Mainland of China, citizenship has traditionally been rooted in a strong sense of morality that has been primarily promoted through citizenship education from the earliest times of Chinese history, to today's People's Republic of China (PRC) (Qin 2014).

Fairbrother (2014) suggests that Chinese rule naturally adopts a paternalistic model, with a basis in the classical works of Confucius. Specifically, this approach views the law as an expression of and secondary to morality. The leader and government officials are expected to lead morally exemplary lives and lead the people to moral behaviour through their own example, as well as through education. Civic education in contemporary China is concerned with promoting a socialist view of life and values such as honesty, integrity, patriotism, care for others and a spirit of service (Qin 2014). Notwithstanding differences in political ideology, Chinese citizenship education, much like citizenship education in other cultural contexts, seeks to promote a sense of civic responsibility towards the country and society, emphasising additionally family responsibility. This notion of shared values and a sense of social responsibility is evident also in citizenship education in the United States, France, the United Kingdom, Singapore and Germany, to name but a few (Wang, 2003; Qin 2005; Qin, Du and Chen 2009).

An international survey of citizenship education in 3,800 schools across twenty-four countries found significant areas of agreement among principals and teachers with regard to the key aims of civic and citizenship education (Schulz et al. 2016). The aims that principals considered to be the most important were promoting students' critical and independent thinking (64 per cent), promoting students' knowledge of citizens' rights and responsibilities (61 per cent) and developing students' skills and competencies in conflict resolution (44 per cent). Meanwhile, teachers also deemed the most important aims as promoting students' independent and critical thinking (61 per cent) and their knowledge of citizens' rights and responsibilities (57 per cent) (Schulz et al. 2016).

While education for citizenship is eagerly promoted by governments and educators across a range of contexts and subjects, questions necessarily arise regarding the tension between promoting a notion of a critically reflective citizenry and the requirement to adhere to a form of morality determined by the state. This tension has been exemplified, for instance, in legal cases that have arisen as a result of differing viewpoints on, for instance, same-sex marriage in contexts such as the United Kingdom, the United States and others. It can also be clearly seen for instance in relation to other concepts, like that of loyalty, that lies at the heart of the oath required for naturalisation to national citizenship, for instance, in the United Kingdom:

> I will give my loyalty to the United Kingdom and respect its rights and freedoms. I will uphold its democratic values. I will observe its laws faithfully and fulfil my duties and obligations as a British citizen.

the United States:

> I hereby declare, on oath, that I absolutely and entirely renounce and abjure all allegiance and fidelity to any foreign prince, potentate, state, or sovereignty, of

> whom or which I have heretofore been a subject or citizen; that I will support and defend the Constitution and laws of the United States of America against all enemies, foreign and domestic; that I will bear true faith and allegiance to the same; that I will bear arms on behalf of the United States when required by the law; that I will perform non-combatant service in the Armed Forces of the United States when required by the law; that I will perform work of national importance under civilian direction when required by the law; and that I take this obligation freely, without any mental reservation or purpose of evasion; so help me God.

South Africa:

> I, [name], do hereby solemnly declare that I will be loyal to the Republic of South Africa, promote all that will advance it and oppose all that may harm it, uphold and respect its Constitution and commit myself to the furtherance of the ideals and principles contained therein.

or the Philippines, to name just a few places:

> I, (name), solemnly swear (or affirm) that I will support and defend the Constitution of the Republic of the Philippines and obey the laws and legal orders promulgated by the duly constituted authorities of the Philippines and I hereby declare that I recognize and accept the supreme authority of the Philippines and will maintain true faith and allegiance thereto; and that I imposed this obligation upon myself voluntarily without mental reservation or purpose of evasion. So help me God.

It is not difficult to see why many nation states may consider an oath of allegiance a necessary requirement for foreigners desirous to become their citizens; yet it is also not difficult to imagine future situations where, due to changing social trends, such unquestioning promises of loyalty to the state may include ideas in conflict with the notion of citizens who are able to make critically reflective choices and decisions with regards to moral standards. Furthermore, the existence of a utopian state acting always for the good of the people is aleatory at best. Thus, the imperative to act as a socially responsible citizen may not always easily align with the notion of full obedience to the state. These eventually opposed aims may come to make it difficult to conceptualise a clear and coherent programme of citizenship education that is distinct from ideological or political education. Indeed, even if it were possible to conceivably address such tensions at the level of national citizenship, the regional and cosmopolitan citizenship education presents further challenges. If, for instance loyalty is considered a core concept of citizenship, as suggested by the oaths seen above, then the question becomes what that loyalty might look like beyond national borders, not least when different forms of citizenship call for behaviours that may conflict with one another. Not only this, but loyalty may be contingent on a sense of group membership. This sense of membership is difficult enough to foster within nation states given the degree of cultural and linguistic diversity characterising today's societies. At regional and global levels the challenge is further compounded, particularly where citizenship is not contingent on a shared history or shared values or where relationships between member states are in themselves strained due to political or economic disagreements, as has been the case for the Arab League in past years. In addition to this, notions of political participation and active citizenship that are, in different forms, present in citizenship conceptualisations across nation states, become difficult to operationalise with regard to supra-national citizenship, either regional or, even more so, cosmopolitan citizenship.

Political participation depends greatly on the existence and accessibility of participatory structures and mechanisms. In the context of supra-national regional and cosmopolitan citizenship political participation is limited, firstly, by a lack of a clearly defined domain within which political participation can take place and, secondly, by the challenge of finding a common ground between nation states and the cumbersome processes that surround joint decision-making, as evidenced for example by the European Union.

Thus, concepts of these regional or cosmopolitan citizenships remain ambiguous, making it difficult for teachers to know what education for such citizenships might consist of or might look like in their professional practice. Further, as discussed previously, the notion of citizenship by definition seems to assume a community on the basis of shared values, since it is only in such contexts that the individual can feasibly exercise civic rights and responsibilities in a legitimate and legitimised way. Yet, it is difficult to envision how this might apply at a global scale, as in the case of cosmopolitan citizenship. It is interesting to note that the IEA study into civic education (Schulz et al. 2016) found that while teachers in most participating countries felt confident addressing certain areas of civic education, there was a widespread lack of confidence with regards to issues relating to the global community, international organisations or emigration and immigrational issues. The researchers hypothesised that this may be due to the kind of training teachers receive for civic-related subjects or perhaps to the period of time when they received their training.

Clear understanding of what it means to be a citizen within any given sphere, or at least of the skills and competencies that constitute effective citizenship within those different spheres, is essential for enabling the translation of the abstract concept of citizenship to tangible educational objectives and practices. Yet, the first step perhaps would be to revisit the very purpose of citizenship education, whether to develop critical thinking that leads to reflective citizenship practice, or whether to promote a notion of loyalty and adherence to a set of moral values, or, perhaps, a little of each of those. A view of education as a tool contributing to the formation of citizens assumes in many cases a top-down model of citizenship that does not always sit easily with notions of critical and reflective thinking. Thus, a question at the heart of any citizenship education initiatives might be whether the vision of society towards which such initiatives are working is one that is organised from the top down, one that is generated from the bottom up or one that is co-constructed through an interplay of both. If the latter, then the next question would be to consider how this interplay unfolds.

This chapter has reflected on some of the challenges and opportunities entailed in conceptualising citizenship at various levels of abstraction from more bounded to less bounded forms. It has examined key assumptions that underpin concepts of citizenship across cultural contexts.

More importantly, it has undertaken a brief examination of the relationship between education and citizenship, including also a sketch of possible tensions between, on the one hand, aspirations to promote a sense of national loyalty and, on the other hand, conceptualisations of critical and reflective citizenship. The discussions further highlight the need for greater definitional clarity to inform education policy and teacher preparation, if the relationship between education and citizenship is to be an even more productive one.

**For reflection**

- While the concept of cosmopolitan citizenship gathers momentum, current socio-political trends show a move towards separatism. To what extent do you think these seemingly opposing directions can co-exist? Or would one inevitably have to give way to the other?
- How might language educators respond to such, or similar, shifts?

Chapter 2

# Theorising the relationship between language education and citizenship

**Objectives**

- To understand how institutional discourse has come to position language education and citizenship as collaborators.
- To critically examine the extent to which these policies are supported by the view of language teaching and learning presented in the literature.
- To examine language teaching and learning through an intercultural communicative competence lens to identify shared values between language and citizenship education.

## INTRODUCTION

Policy at the national, supra-national and global levels has for some time promoted an association between foreign language education and citizenship, as we have seen in Chapter 1. Academic literature has also theorised the relationship between language education and citizenship as a mutually beneficial one: foreign language teaching offers a unique entry point for key citizenship themes and issues, most obviously in the context of intercultural and global citizenship, while citizenship practices provide a social purpose for language learning, through which language learning becomes meaningful and relevant. It is interesting to note that within most countries' requirements for foreign nationals to be able to acquire citizenship, there is the need to pass an examination in the language and culture of the host country. This makes evident the link between language learning and the practice of citizenship.

Language can be viewed as the *medium* through which citizens realise, express and shape their role in civic society (Breidbach 2002), as well as a *context* within which learners can engage with multiple identities and develop appreciation of and respect for diversity, in turn impacting on the ways in which they view the world and their place within it, and this is recognised in policy also:

> It is widely accepted that learning a new language can give the learner insights into how other people think, and engender respect for other cultures and ways of life. It can lead to more tolerant attitudes on a broader front and to respect for

other institutions and values, both within the UK and in the wider world. (The Nuffield Foundation 2000: 30)

Even across contexts that share the same official first language, this same language can communicate very different social realities and experiences. The United Kingdom, the United States, Canada, Australia, New Zealand, Ireland, all share the same language, English, and yet they represent distinct and diverse societies. Language becomes the means through which these realities and experiences are expressed and lived.

## LANGUAGE TEACHING AND POLITICAL CITIZENSHIP

Two primary arguments can be made for intertwining citizenship and language teaching. The first focuses on the political nature of citizenship, encompassing awareness of and engagement with processes and structures for political participation, while the second emphasises the social, referring largely to an active participation in pursuits such as volunteer programmes, social enterprises, etc., with an aim to contribute to social change and enhancement. In both cases, language is seen as the means through which identity is shaped and citizenship is enacted. Through language, individuals negotiate their sense of self across contexts and time frames and gain access to the social structures through which they are able to speak and have a voice (Norton 2013). Aligning herself with Foucault (1980), Norton (2013) proposes that language teaching is a highly political practice entailing power relations that operate both at the macro level of legal or social welfare systems and at the micro level of social encounters between people with differing access to material resources. Encounters and practices at both levels are produced with and through language (Norton 2013: 47), placing language at the heart of citizenship enactment across the social, political and civic arenas. Weedon (1997) succinctly expresses very similar ideas: 'Language is the place where actual and possible forms of social organization and their likely social and political consequences are defined and contested. Yet it is also the place where our sense of ourselves, our subjectivity, is constructed' (p. 21).

European citizenship is one case where linguistic competence plays a clear role in making accessible the political aspects of citizenship and in their realisation. Breidbach (2002) argues for the development of European citizenship through language teaching, positing that the creation of and participation in political spaces of public discourse by European citizens is, at the most basic level, accessed through languages. Democratic legitimacy more broadly can be argued since its Athenian creation to be based on the exchange of information and opinion, requiring not only cultural and political literacy but also the linguistic ability to participate in such discourse (Breidbach 2002). On the other hand, linguistic competence is integral also to social and cultural practices in the multilingual and multicultural societies in today's world.

## LANGUAGE TEACHING AND SOCIAL CITIZENSHIP

Language learning has been in the spotlight of discussions of citizenship and citizenship education. In the United Kingdom, for instance, the Nuffield Foundation undertook a seminal examination of the language learning situation. Its report supported the promotion of language learning as a means of fostering tolerance and respect, citing its potential to give learners new insights into how other people think, and to engender respect for other cultures and ways of life. Indeed, the UK-based report argued that more effective language learning could help to combat the insular outlook, with which the United Kingdom is often charged (Rojek 2008) and which has received particular criticism following the Brexit referendum result.

On the one hand, research evidence supports the idea that exposure to other cultures, particularly through periods of study abroad, can promote intercultural competence (e.g. Ramirez 2016). However, closer examination points to the importance of conscious pedagogical efforts and intentional intercultural education in optimising the intercultural learning that takes place during the study abroad period (Behrnd and Porzelt 2012; Young and Schartner 2014; Schartner 2016). Thus, in and of itself exposure to cultural diversity may not go far enough in promoting intercultural competence. Instead, such exposure should be accompanied by opportunities for critical analysis and discussion and 'active processing' of intercultural encounters (Peckenpaugh 2012). The language classroom offers a context for engaging learners with an alternative set of cultural values and a different way of understanding the world (Byram 1992; Advisory Group on the Teaching of Citizenship and Democracy in Schools (1998). Through this engagement learners have the opportunity to critically examine their own and other values and worldviews, and to develop the competencies that lie at the heart of reaping all the benefits available from intercultural citizenship. In this process of language learning, learners become familiar with a new form of expression and a context for negotiating a range of identities (Norton 2000). This negotiation process reflects the demands of today's culturally diverse societies, such that language classrooms become an arena for supporting and guiding learners in reconciling multiple identities at all levels of citizenship.

Common to language teaching and citizenship education is the importance of embracing and enacting multiple identities across cultural settings and groups and a desire to actively participate in today's culturally diverse societies (Osler and Starkey 2005b). How far these aims are achieved is crucial in determining the extent to which citizenship practices contribute towards social cohesion. Yet, the development of citizenship through language learning requires a form of language teaching that not only exposes learners to cultural diversity but also equips them with the tools for critically engaging with different worldviews and ways of life. In this fullest form, language teaching promotes diversity as an integral and enriching aspect of society and equips learners to better understand the value of their own and other cultural values, drawing on the best of all of them. Nevertheless, it is true that the diversity of philosophies and values represented in today's societies, while stimulating, is also challenging. Negotiating an appreciation of rich cultural diversity, and critical evaluation of the relative merits of diverse value frameworks, requires a willingness to engage with complexity as well as the skills of critical analysis and reflection. Without doubt there are times when value frameworks strongly oppose one another, and only *or* the other leads to the flourishing of individuals and society. Thus, the critically engaged yet interculturally competent citizen is called upon to discern the values that lead to social harmony and individual flourishing within a framework of respect for cultural diversity. Eriksen (2006) suggests that while 'difference' can be viewed as creating conflict or distance between individuals and communities, 'diversity' can be seen instead as providing cultural and social enrichment.

While such a clear-cut distinction may work better in theory than in practice, it nevertheless acknowledges the tension between identifying the strengths that diverse cultures bring to society and recognising that certain notions and practices may work against social cohesion and human welfare. The Crick Report (1998) echoes this sentiment, taking the view that, while diversity is positive and enriching, difference is a reality with which citizens must contend. Language learning provides a context for engendering and promoting appreciation of and respect for diversity, the willingness to step outside of one's comfort zone and engage with other worldviews, the skills of critical reflection on one's own cultural identity and those of others, and the exposure to and practice of linguistic repertoires through which to shape and enact civic participation.

## LANGUAGE TEACHING FOR BUILDING COMMUNITY

A key aspect of the practice of citizenship is social participation in a shared endeavour and a sense of membership in the community that drives a desire to contribute meaningfully to that community. Language is considered the primary tool for preserving and transmitting culture, 'linking individuals into communities of shared identity' (Phillipson 1992: 79). Within each of these communities, language defines boundaries of inclusion and exclusion into membership of a single speech community and acts as a tool for social identification providing linguistic markers that indicate social stratification (Saville-Troike 2003). Through the development of multilingual repertoires, it can also act as the means through which different speech communities can come together, breaking down unhelpful stratifications, while consolidating and extending to other groups the effects of helpful ones. Social development and the perpetuation of culture rely on the preservation of history and a knowledge base for future generations, passed down through the medium of language (Crystal 1997). Thus, language is instrumental in socialisation processes, offering the means through which we manage political, economic and social structures and through which we express emotion and verbalise our thoughts. Furthermore, the linguistic repertoire of a society plays a key part in shaping and defining that society, as is clearly evident in the way nations determine their official language(s) and the consequences this has in the possible ascendancy of certain linguistic groups over others. Similarly, the decision of which languages are taught in schools has typically been a result of political and historical relations, rather than a reflection of the social reality of language learners. Convery et al. (1997), for instance, highlighted the fact that the persistent focus in England on the teaching of French, German and, in rare cases, Italian limited the extent to which teachers could offer pupils a broad insight into the full reach of European citizenship and membership of that community. Indeed, the argument could be extended further, given that cosmopolitan citizenship in today's world would greatly be enhanced by linguistic competence in non-European languages, not least Mandarin Chinese or Arabic.

## LANGUAGE TEACHING FOR THE MULTIPLICITY OF CITIZENSHIP

As discussed in Chapter 1, citizenship can be viewed as a combination of *rights*, *access* and *belonging* (Bellamy 2008); the importance of language education to be able to understand rights, to access institutions and situations and to belong to the country and its culture is paramount. At its simplest level citizenship is a legal status conferred upon members of a given grouping, establishing a legal relationship between the individual and the state. However, the blossoming field of citizenship education sets out a more ambitious conceptualisation of citizenship bringing with it not only knowledge and understanding of rights and responsibilities leading to active social participation, but also values of tolerance and respect, a critical consideration of commonality and difference, and a shared understanding of, and respect for, human dignity and the flourishing of society.

Central to the conceptualisation of education for cosmopolitan and intercultural citizenship education is the notion of the individual who is able to engage critically with social and political processes and to participate in these processes in a principled and informed way, demonstrating respect for diversity in all its guises and evidencing an ability to evaluate strengths and weaknesses in such a way that the individual is enabled to preserve and further social progress. Active citizenship in this sense is widely considered to be at the core of democratic, participative society and requires a systematic approach to ensure that citizens are not only aware of their rights but are also able to exercise them effectively and in line with their freedom to choose the kind of identity they wish to enact.

Two basic key tools in promoting active citizenship can be said to be education and language. It is education that equips citizens with the knowledge and understanding of social processes and language with which they can (a) access the necessary further education and knowledge, and (b) effectively communicate their views and needs, call local and national governments to account and access membership of social groupings, etc. Language provides the medium through which citizens can realise and express their role in civic society, participate in social processes and shape society.

The relationship between language and citizenship becomes more intricate when identity is brought into play. Put simply, our tendency to play an active civic role in social and political processes is dependent to a large degree on the extent to which we see our citizenship as part of our identity. In other words, if our citizenship marks us out as members of a given group and if we consider this to be an important aspect of our identity, we are more likely to have a greater desire to contribute meaningfully to that given group. Conversely, the more actively we participate in social and political processes that characterise a given social grouping, the more likely we are to consider ourselves part of that group thus strengthening our group identity.

Language learning plays a key role in taking the learner beyond local and national identities and across multiple identities, to see themselves as part of a wider social grouping wherein, equipped with the necessary tools, they can play their part in shaping their society. Today's language learners can be said to hold multiple citizenships; whether local, national or global. Through language learning the individual is offered access to social groupings in all these citizenship domains, allowing them to understand and play their part in each. As understandings of citizenship shift from the national to the cosmopolitan in response to the changing global context, language education needs to take learners beyond simply the acquisition of vocabulary and grammar, promoting instead a critical understanding of other cultures and ways of life together with a critical reflection on self-identity that enables learners to understand their roles more fully. While the Hansard Society, the British Youth Council and the Citizenship Advisory Group unanimously agree that citizenship education programmes should encourage tolerance and respect for individuals *irrespective* of gender, race, culture or religion, language teaching for citizenship development needs to engage with difference and diversity, viewing diversity not as something to be set aside but to be valued and appreciated, and difference as something to be understood and negotiated.

## CITIZENSHIP, FOREIGN LANGUAGE LEARNING AND INTERCULTURAL COMMUNICATIVE COMPETENCE

The need for cross-cultural understanding has existed for as long as civilised societies, with the need for appropriate ambassadors who could mediate between linguistic or culturally diverse groups being at the heart of successful diplomatic relationships (Byram 1997). Rapid shifts towards globalisation in recent decades have resulted in increased accessibility to cross-linguistic and cross-cultural interactions to those outside the diplomatic or professional fields. This expansion has motivated national and supra-national bodies to call for language education to equip learners for effective cross-cultural understanding and communication (e.g. the Nuffield Language Inquiry 2000; the House of Lords European Union Select Committee 2005; Commission of the European Communities 2008). Rapid innovation in language teaching during the nineteenth and twentieth centuries, due in part to demands from industrialisation and globalisation, saw a shift in some contexts away from traditional grammar-translation approaches considering them to be incommensurate with the communicative purposes of a changing society and a changing world. In many world contexts, however, grammar-translation methods continue to be the mainstay. In both cases, language policy has come to recognise, either explicitly or by implication, the increasing need for culturally appropriate language use to generate effective cross-cultural communication and intercultural understanding. In this development, we see firstly the important role that language learning plays in equipping citizens to adequately respond to social, economic and political realities on the global stage. The role of language learning in the development of cultural and intercultural understanding lies at the heart of this. As a consequence, the foreign language teacher becomes instrumental in introducing the learner not simply to a new linguistic system but to another socio-political and cultural reality. This shifting understanding of language learning has resulted also in evolving conceptualisations of *culture*, in turn impacting on language pedagogy.

In the context of language teaching, culture can be conceptualised in two primary ways (Kramsch 1995). The first focuses on the representation social groups generate of themselves and others through what can be termed their 'material productions', namely 'works of art, literature, social institutions, or artefacts of everyday life, and the mechanisms for their reproduction and preservation through history' (1995: 84). The second refers to 'the attitudes and beliefs, ways of thinking, behaving and remembering shared by members of that community' (Nostrand 1989: 51, cited in Kramsch 1995) and can be referred to as 'culture as a social practice'. The first conceptualisation gave rise to a study of culture through classical texts, understanding the present and imagining the future in light of the past. This approach emphasises the centrality of 'high' culture or 'Culture with a Capital C', focusing on the teaching of literature, the arts, music, and so on, of the target culture.

The second approach focuses on observation and data gathering, understanding the present by viewing current events in light of their social diversity and their relation to other contemporary events. This conceptualisation of culture is at the heart of intercultural communicative competence (ICC). Byram's (1997) widely-recognised model of ICC proposes five key competencies as central to the development of ICC: *savoir comprendre* (skills of interpreting and relating), *savoir* (knowledge of self and other), *savoir s'engager* (political education and critical cultural awareness), *savoir être* (relativising the self and valuing the other), and *savoir apprendre/faire* (skills of discovery and interaction). According to Byram and his colleagues, mastery of these *saviors*, or know-hows, constitutes the basis of effective intercultural citizenship. Fantini (2000) also talks of five key competencies for successful intercultural communication: awareness, attitudes, skills, knowledge and language proficiency. He further suggests that the effective intercultural speaker must exhibit specific attributes – respect, empathy, flexibility, patience, interest, curiosity, openness, motivation, a sense of humour, tolerance for ambiguity – and would also benefit from a willingness to suspend judgement (2000: 28).

An emphasis on skills or competencies implies a reconceptualisation of culture, from an emphasis on history, literature, philosophy and the arts to a dynamic, shared way of life, viewing individuals as social agents who shape and are shaped by cultural practices, values and understandings. Byram, Gribkova and Starkey (2002: 5) propose that the intercultural dimension of language teaching should seek to develop *intercultural speakers* or *mediators* able to engage with complexity and multiple identities and to avoid the stereotyping that accompanies perceiving someone through a single identity. Developing this dimension of language learning requires learners to perceive the interlocutor as an individual whose qualities are to be discovered, rather than representing an externally ascribed identity. While 'high' culture is seen to represent an 'externally ascribed identity', instead the focus shifts to learners developing an understanding of multiple identities to be discovered through interaction. Through this lens, the concept of ICC may be considered to be central to the fostering of a closer relationship between citizenship and language teaching. ICC begins from the premise that a key aim of language teaching is the development of the skills necessary for effective citizenship practices in today's multicultural society, examples of which might be the linguistic means through which to establish and develop contact with other cultural and linguistic groups. ICC could then can be argued to be the conceptual link between language teaching and citizenship development. In learning a language, learners transition from the familiar to the unfamiliar and in that process they are required to interpret, relate to and interact with alternative value frameworks and worldviews.

The arguments we have reviewed present a view of foreign language teaching that encourages learners towards critical evaluation of value sets in their own and other cultures. In this view, the core purpose of language learning is to facilitate dialogue and interaction. Participation in social and political processes is also part of this equation, while the content of language teaching seeks to enable learners to engage with principles of an appreciation and respect for cultural diversity and a sense of intercultural belonging that engenders meaningful civic participation. Much of the literature argues that through developing an understanding and appreciation of other ways of life, the intercultural aspect of language teaching makes an essential contribution to education for active democratic citizenship, whether at a national, supra-national or global level (e.g. Guilherme 2002; Byram 2014).

Citizenship and language learning share the goals of addressing learners' identities and promoting and developing skills for intercultural communication and participation. Given the intertwined nature of language, identity, group membership and citizenship, language learning and citizenship have been theorised as ideal companions (Osler and Starkey 2005b). Language teaching has been put forward as a key means through which learners might be equipped with the necessary skills for effective citizenship practice in multicultural societies. Two key premises underpin such a proposal: firstly, language provides a window to other ways of life, enabling learners to critically engage with their own and other worldviews; secondly, language provides and enables the primary means through which to express participation in social and political structures that mark out identity and group membership. Thus, language learning enables participation beyond the immediate community, extending local citizenship to include a cosmopolitan citizenship. ICC provides a useful framework for understanding the relationship between language learning and citizenship and for organising the pathways through which this relationship might transfer to practice. The extent to which language teachers consider themselves the 'foreign language and intercultural competence teacher' (Sercu 2006) will decisively impact on learners' engagement with the new culture. Subsequent chapters consider whether and to what degree this notion is currently a classroom reality.

This chapter has examined the rationale for drawing close relationships between citizenship development and language teaching. In the contemporaneous context of increased social diversity and mass transnational mobility, the need for intercultural communication skills that promote social cohesion enabling individuals to work together for common goals has arguably never been more important. Language education as a means through which learners engage with other identities, worldviews and language systems for communicating and negotiating meaning is argued to be in a unique position to contribute to the development of a more committed practice of citizenship.

**For reflection**

- To what extent do you think it is the role of the language teacher to promote intercultural competence?
- To what extent do you think language can be taught without addressing learners' intercultural awareness? What might such teaching look like and what might be the purposes and consequences of such practice?

# Chapter 3

# Multilingualism and citizenship

**Objectives**

- To engage with conceptualisations of multilingualism.
- To develop an awareness of how citizenship relates to multilingualism in the higher education domain.
- To critically evaluate the relationship between citizenship education and language learning.
- To critically examine the nexus between conceptualisations of multilingualism and citizenship.

## INTRODUCTION

In Chapter 1 we sought to raise awareness of key conceptualisations of citizenship that will underpin much of the discussion to follow. We also highlighted the potentially transformative role of education, and specifically languages education, in developing individuals' knowledge and understanding of active citizenship to facilitate their engagement with society at this level.

We now move on to introduce the concepts of multilingualism and multiculturalism, in order to explore their relationships with (active) citizenship. Furthermore, we then seek to identify how these notions relate to social cohesion. We will outline different perspectives on multilingualism and multiculturalism, that is to say those who consider these concepts as a challenge (something negative), and those who take them to be an opportunity (something positive). We consider how multilingualism and citizenship interact in higher education settings, as well as in language learning environments. We explore some key tenets of citizenship education, and raise for reflection some possible parallels between language education and citizenship education. We conclude by posing some points for reflection on the interconnectivity between multilingualism and citizenship.

## CONCEPTUALISING MULTILINGUALISM

We open with coverage of different conceptualisations of multilingualism and multilingual repertoires that have been expressed in the literature to date, in order to set the scene for discussions of citizenship, multilingual repertoires and (in)equality, language and citizenship education, and social cohesion. As a starting point, what will be dealt with here are ways in which both 'elite' and 'non-elite' bilingualism, as well as 'additive' and 'subtractive' bilingualism have been defined. While traditionally these may well have been established as oppositional constructs, the current stance in much literature is that they are better conceptualised as being ends of a continuum (Geurrero 2010: 166). This will then lead to coverage of current work on translanguaging, and its greater focus on an integrated, holistic linguistic repertoire, and individual agency.

Considering firstly elite and non-elite bilingualism, Guerrero (2010: 167–168) outlines that the contrast between the two rests on the degree of necessity felt in developing a bilingual repertoire. Under this paradigm, both of the authors having had the opportunity to pursue university degrees in foreign languages would represent elite bilingualism for example, as we are developing a bilingual (or indeed a multilingual) repertoire primarily for the sake of personal interest and development. On the other hand, for an individual engaging in language learning due to acute necessity (for example, immigrants, or displaced persons, who arrive in a new country and must learn the host language(s) in order to cope with life in that environment), this would come under the category of non-elite bilingualism, or 'folk' bilingualism to use the term favoured by other authors. We use these examples simply to illustrate the contrast established in the literature.

Additive and subtractive bilingualism is a somewhat related pair of concepts to elite and non-elite but refers rather to the multilingual repertoire a person develops and maintains as a result of language learning. Additive bilingualism, according to Lo Bianco (2010: 23), is where the new language learned sits alongside any previously acquired languages (including, crucially, mother tongue(s)), rather than replacing them. The previously acquired languages remain a substantial and valued part of the individual's repertoire. Subtractive bilingualism defines a situation where the new language plays an increasingly dominant role in relation to the existing ones, and as Lo Bianco (2010: 23) points out, this is often true for minority communities in a new host context, learning what he terms the 'dominant' language of the majority, and, gradually, competence in the first language(s) is lost. With reference to the Australian context, Lo Bianco gives the examples of both immigrant and indigenous populations' language practices being characterised as subtractive bilingualism.

Links can be drawn, then, between elite and additive bilingualism, as well as between non-elite and subtractive bilingualism. In the context of industrialised nations at least, elite bilingualism has often typically referred to language learning practices engaged in by majority, established, relatively privileged individuals, who do so in order to enhance their linguistic repertoire through adding a further language(s); individuals occupying a less privileged position in a society may not engage in becoming bi/multilingual for its own sake necessarily, and various circumstances can often lead to the original language competences being lost, hence subtractive (for example, families seeking to support children's development of the new language, in order to encourage social and academic adjustment at school, by speaking it rather than the first language in the home, thus potentially leading to eventual loss of the latter; for a detailed exploration of parents' views on the links between language use and their child's social integration in the school context, see Evans et al. 2016). As Guerrero explains,

> Elite bilinguals acquire another language and maintain their L1, as happens in additive bilingualism . . . Their L2 embodies an advantage in social and economic terms. Folk or circumstantial bilingualism could be associated with subtractive bilingualism in that individuals acquire an L2 and tend to lose the L1 because the latter has low prestige in the context where the individuals live; hence, a likely consequence of subtractive is monolingualism (García, 1997; Martin-Jones, 2007; Valdés and Figueroa, 1994). (Guerrero 2010: 168–169)

It is important to remember however that contextual differences can lead to these terms being interpreted and ascribed in various ways. Guerrero (2010: 171) believes it vital to understand context-specific policies and practices around the world in order to best grasp how the terms apply. Furthermore, Rydenvald's (2015) work on multilingual children attending international schools aims to bring into question the notion of 'elite' bilingualism, arguing that her participant group of interest has been largely overlooked in previous research, given that the multilingual repertoires of those who are seen as 'privileged' (such as children in international schools) are believed to be 'unproblematic' (Rydenvald 2015: 214). She attempts to highlight how multilingualism is necessarily complex, multifaceted and, indeed, potentially 'problematic' in any given context, noting, for example, that many of her questionnaire respondents report strongly valuing and frequently using their home language of Swedish, as well as English, but less so the majority language in their country of residence. Rydenvald posits that this is perhaps because of the 'elite' nature of their bilingualism (one might infer that this connects to points made above about 'necessity' or otherwise of an individual to learn another language), and that to engage to a greater extent with the local language would further enhance their linguistic repertoire.

The apparent fluidity and context-specific nature of these conceptualisations of bilingualism connect with a recent paradigm shift in the field of applied linguistics towards 'translanguaging', which is an attempt to break down the traditionally reified, fixed and distinct notion of languages themselves, viewing them instead as intimately interrelated entities within a multilingual individual's holistic repertoire (Otheguy, García and Reid 2015), so that there is 'a focus on the agency of individuals engaged in using, creating, and interpreting signs for communication' (Creese and Blackledge 2015: 26). Creese and Blackledge, further, seek to emphasise what they call the 'transformative' power of this approach, which leads to a dismantling of pervasive beliefs about the relative importance or value of different languages, both within an individual's repertoire, but also within a society (ibid.). Those subscribing to a translanguaging paradigm accept the helpfulness of a departure from 'abstract, idealized notions of "a language" as a set of skills', to emphasise and appreciate instead the way multilingualism can be deployed in everyday interaction (Creese and Blackledge, 2015: 27). Canagarajah, another seminal proponent of the translanguaging paradigm (see for example Canagarajah 2011: 401–402), argues that there is an as yet limited body of research into how translanguaging practices can be facilitated and supported in order for students to benefit from them. One of his particular areas of focus (2011) is translanguaging practices in the university context: it is to the theme of language practices in internationalisation in higher education that we turn next, making explicit links to citizenship at the global level.

## MULTILINGUALISM, CITIZENSHIP AND HIGHER EDUCATION

This section turns to questions of citizenship in the context of internationalisation of higher education. The literature in this domain tends to talk about 'global citizenship' (so far, we have tended to use the term 'cosmopolitan citizenship' in our discussions of citizenship beyond the national level; Chapter 7 seeks to compare and contrast this often overlapping terminology), and what emerges from this body of work are strong arguments in favour of citizenship being fostered in the university context, and indeed linguistic issues arising from this as well.

Vandrick (e.g. 1995) has discussed extensively the complexities of navigating class- and race-based issues and identities within an education setting, and has argued strongly for the importance of explicitly engaging with debate surrounding these themes, rather than choosing to ignore them (Vandrick, 1995: 377). Failure to acknowledge these issues is tantamount, she says, to enabling privileged and elite individuals to maintain such a status, rather than actively seeking to work towards a 'more genuine equity' (ibid.). Parallels between this discussion, and the treatment above of elite and non-elite bilingualism, are clear – failure to address the processes and ideologies behind these different kinds of bilingualism, with their relative levels of status, will merely perpetuate such inequalities for generations to come. For teachers and learners to work together in different education settings, from primary and secondary up to tertiary levels, to value a range of multilingual repertoires represented in the classroom, could be a way to address this.

Canagarajah's work is a tangible example of this: through a translanguaging lens he analysed a university student's written work – a student for whom English is a second language – to best evaluate the creativity inherent in the work, as well as to raise for debate where certain elements of the written production sits on a continuum from 'mistakes' to 'codemeshing', and indeed how both instructors and students should conceptualise 'deviations' from recognised standards and norms in academic writing, potentially seeing them as positive rather than negative elements. Reflecting on this process, he says:

> There are good reasons why we should develop teaching practices from the strategies learners themselves use. Multilingual students bring from their homes

> and communities funds of knowledge that are valuable for themselves and others (Gonzalez, Moll, & Amanti, 2005). It is important for teachers to learn from them rather than impose their own views of how codemeshing works. (Canagarajah 2011: 415)

This discussion of international students' multilingual repertoires – and the extent to which they are valued and acknowledged against a backdrop of higher education institutions having established norms and standards in formal academic writing and speaking – brings us explicitly to a consideration of global citizenship within this same context. Recently, there has been a turn to focus on such issues of citizenship within the domain of internationalisation of higher education, and one example of this is work by Haigh (2014). Covering issues relating to international students' 'vulnerability' (2014: 9), Haigh highlights the problem of the linguistic and cultural repertoires of these students not being valued by the host institution, and various stakeholders within. Haigh's discussion of the perceived problems of 'difference', be it linguistic, cultural, educational or social, introduces us to ways in which individuals may exhibit wariness of the notion of the 'other', and of multiplicity, and there being a focus from certain institutions or individuals on the need for incomers to 'integrate', which is to say to adhere to a fixed way of doing things (these ideas are dealt with in depth later on in this chapter). Haigh makes it clear that these are highly pertinent issues facing processes of internationalisation in higher education today. Particularly relevant to our discussion here is Haigh's focus on the potential role of 'education for global citizenship', as a way of better understanding internationalisation, to move away from beliefs about incoming students being 'deficient' (ibid.):

> Education for global citizenship is about learning to live together sustainably (Delors, 1996). No longer about competition; this is a more idealistic and communitarian notion and it marks a major step change in thinking about internationalisation and its purpose in higher education. (Haigh 2014: 13)

Crucially, he says, education for global citizenship is about inclusion, empathy, and informed and insightful evaluation of received norms, in order to better appreciate the value in alternative viewpoints and behaviours: '[citizens of the world] should respect its limits and the rights of all its inhabitants, current, and future, and accept their personal responsibilities for the welfare of all' (Haigh 2014: 14). Gacel-Ávila (2005: 125) agrees that university teaching and learning underpinned by an internationalisation aspect should primarily be about fostering an appreciation of diversity, rendering global citizens who are 'defenders of democratic principles of their society, and true architects of social change', which links to earlier discussions of active citizenship being promoted through education. She outlines the substantial benefits she believes can be accrued by students exposed to an internationalised learning environment:

> . . . when students leave their own cultural environment – for study abroad or academic programs based on intercultural communication techniques with

> content that highlights the international and global dimension of human and social interaction – they have the possibility to develop a capacity for adaptation and flexibility as they are faced with rapidly changing situations and the opportunity to broaden their cultural and intellectual horizons and to adapt to different kinds of people. (Gacel-Ávila, 2005: 127–128)

While we strongly agree with how rich an internationalised education experience is for developing a sense of global citizenship, and indeed individuals who identify as global citizens, we raise the concern that this is something that can only be accessed by those who have the means to travel abroad to seek such experience, as Gacel-Ávila seems to suggest. Perry et al. (2016: 345) have also emphasised the role played by studying abroad in the development of global citizenship: '[. . .] exposure to new places, cultures, and learning environments where a student's preconceived and established notions and beliefs are tested, may act as the catalyst or impetus to bring forth a transformative experience'.

We propose that the inevitable inequity that results from this means there are potentially millions of individuals around the world who are not able to access such opportunities for development, reflection and growth, through learning about and contributing to global citizenship. The question arises, therefore, about what opportunities there might be for individuals to explore these same processes, even when the financial means to travel and study abroad are not available (or, indeed, perhaps the question should be what can be done to make studying abroad less financially unattainable for so many?). Perry et al. (2016) propose that for students in the United States seeking study abroad experiences, shorter-term programmes are a more financially accessible way to participate, and the benefits of this international exposure can indeed be accrued at least to some extent even within a much shorter time frame (Perry et al. 2016: 351–352). It should be kept in mind, though, that some students even in relatively wealthy countries will still not be able to afford short-term study opportunities abroad, and certainly there must be high numbers of students in less developed countries around the world for whom accessing any kind of international travel for furthering one's education is likely impossible. It is important to consider these imbalances within a discussion of global citizenship: Ibrahim (2005: 178, drawing on Wringe 1999) explains that 'responsible global citizenship' is necessarily underpinned with a foundation of social justice ideals, which is to say facilitating the improvement in circumstances of some, without simultaneously having a negative effect on others. This is supported also by a tenet of the 1995 UNESCO framework for cosmopolitan citizenship (discussed in Chapter 1), namely 'promoting solidarity and equity at national and international levels' (247).

In this section we have introduced some key principles relating to citizenship, higher education and indeed inequality: we extend the discussion of these themes in Chapter 7. However, we conclude here by returning explicitly to related linguistic issues in higher education. Alongside the developmental benefits accrued by those able to undertake some kind of study abroad could also be linguistic benefits, primarily in terms of improvement of language proficiency (this will often refer to English language, given the dominant trend for individuals across the world to seek higher education opportunities in institutions where programmes are taught through this medium, often those in predominantly English-speaking countries; for an example focusing on study abroad in non-English language contexts see Meier and Daniels 2013). That some individuals are able to access this opportunity for linguistic development and not others again leads to inequality in terms of competitiveness on the job market when such individuals return to their home context (see for example Ianelli and Huang 2014: 807 for discussion of this phenomenon in relation to Chinese students specifically). That, broadly speaking, there is a tendency for there to be a dominance of English-medium education in the context of internationalisation of higher education (Gacel-Ávila 2005: 129, for example, talks about 'linguistic unification through the use of English' in the internationalisation of higher education, without bringing this into question) could mean there is in turn a dominance of various native English-speaking cultures within processes of development of global citizenship. If this is indeed the case, then this would go against the aims, outlined above, of global citizenship education.

## MULTILINGUALISM, CITIZENSHIP AND LANGUAGE LEARNING

Having outlined various theoretical stances on multilingualism, and how multilingualism and citizenship interact in the domain of higher education, we turn now to explore how multilingualism and citizenship interact in settings focused on language learning practices more broadly. Underpinning our discussion is a belief that language learning has a potentially powerful role to play in terms of developing a sense of citizenship; language learning enables diversity to be acknowledged and celebrated (Hennebry 2014: 242).

Already in this chapter we have sought to understand the myriad ways in which multilingualism has been conceptualised, in order to consider how multilingual repertoires interact with issues of elitism, (in)equality, power differentials, ideology and privilege. To extend this discussion, we move now to think about how these issues might interact with conceptualisations of citizenship in the language classroom.

Drawing on arguments from Fishman (e.g. Fishman, Cooper and Conrad 1977), Guerrero raises the issue of how decisions about which language to be learned could offer another, somewhat positive, aspect to elite bilingualism, entitled 'enrichment' bilingualism, where those who are unconstrained in their decision about which language to learn opt for languages spoken by minority groups within society, rather than a more typical option (for example, French, Spanish or German, or more recently also Mandarin, in the United Kingdom). Not only would these individuals benefit from an enhanced and more sensitive and nuanced awareness of their local environment by doing so, Guerrero states, but this would also afford greater support and value to these minority languages themselves, and indeed the multilingual repertoires of those who speak them as first languages. Doing so, in turn, could reinforce the validity of citizenship on the part of individuals who speak minority languages – that is to say, ensuring citizens with a range of diverse multilingual and multicultural repertoires are valued equally in a society.

Fishman's ideas, taken up by Guerrero in 2010 (the latter noting that they have not really gained a great deal of traction in those intervening years), are still being proposed in current times – a professor at the University of Cambridge, Wendy Ayres-Bennett, recently discussed this issue in the British press, arguing for the importance of learning community languages such as Urdu and Polish (also making mention of indigenous languages such as Welsh, Irish and Scottish Gaelic). Not only is it important to encourage English language learning among immigrant communities, but it is just as vital to develop competence in and valuing of immigrants' home languages among other sectors in society: she makes explicit mention on a number of occasions to how this may facilitate social cohesion, explored in the next section. To quote her words from one such news item (entitled '"Brits should learn Polish or Urdu to help encourage integration", says Cambridge linguistics professor'):

> I would like to see more opportunities for British people to learn some of the community languages of the UK, such as Polish, Punjabi and Urdu, particularly in areas where there are high numbers of those speakers, so that there is some mutual effort in understanding the others' language and culture . . . Without English, immigrants are likely to develop exclusive social networks and alternative labour markets . . . We need to respect and celebrate this and to see English as adding to their multilingual and multicultural identities, rather than trying to force immigrants to suppress or even lose their home language and culture. (Care 2017)

Professor Bennett's comments provide a tangible example of subtractive bilingualism in her reflections on the possibility of language loss. It is also worth noting that, in response to Guerrero's point about this stance not really having gathered a lot of support since the era in which Fishman was originally writing, reader comments in response to this argument put forward in the press were very mixed – while some were in support of this view, there were many who were quite taken aback at the suggestion that they might have an active part to play in social cohesion and integration. Often, the view espoused was along the lines of 'you come here to our country, you speak our language'. Such views may link quite closely, it could be argued, to the notion of the language and citizenship of some individuals being valued far more strongly than others. This pattern is also evident in the school domain, both in the languages that are valued and seen as legitimate within the school community in general and those that are formally learned as part of the curriculum. While there are examples of efforts being made to support the role of community languages within schools in general (e.g. De Britos 2016), and indeed instances where pupils are offered the opportunity to sit a formal examination in their home language in order to gain a recognised qualification to represent their skills, there could still be more done in this regard. To return to Creese and Blackledge's (2015) discussion of translanguaging, they suggest that to use this paradigm to underpin pedagogy could better demonstrate the valuing of contributions made by 'language-minoritised students'. They state:

> A translanguaging approach to teaching and learning is not about code-switching, but rather about an arrangement that normalizes bilingualism without diglossic functional separation. Baker (2011, p. 288) defined translanguaging as the process of "meaning making, shaping experiences, gaining understanding and knowledge through the use of two languages". In the classroom, translanguaging approaches draw on all the linguistic resources of the child to maximize understanding and achievement. Thus, both or all languages are used in a dynamic and functionally integrated manner to organize and mediate understanding, speaking, literacy, and learning (Lewis, Jones & Baker, 2012). (Creese and Blackledge, 2015: 26)

Having explored the relationship between multilingualism and citizenship in educational domains from a number of different angles, our attention now turns to citizenship education itself.

## MULTICULTURALISM AND CITIZENSHIP EDUCATION

We have covered substantial ground in our treatment of citizenship and multilingualism, and how their relationship manifests in different educational contexts. In this section we focus our attention explicitly on citizenship education (contrasting with our earlier emphasis on language education) and its interaction with multiculturalism and social cohesion (concepts intertwined with multilingualism).

In Chapter 1 we raised the possibility of citizenship at the national level being founded on an idea of commonly shared principles among those who stake some claim to being part of that nation. Perhaps seemingly paradoxical at first, we identified one key British value, as stated by the Home Office, as 'tolerance of those with different faiths and beliefs' – that is to say, citizens are brought together in the shared pursuit of appreciating and supporting diversity. It is important to critically examine whether this notion of unity through diversity is as contradictory as it first appears. As we explained, engagement with 'active and participatory citizenship' is built upon common principles and beliefs, but raised the possibility of this not existing in certain contexts (that is to say, there instead being divergent views/values which we posited could be either a positive or a negative thing). We argue that some awareness, and indeed critical reflection, of commonalities in values shared among citizens is a useful starting point to then encourage an awareness and appreciation of the value of diversity within a society, in whichever form that may take: here we are concerned primarily with linguistic and cultural diversity. Furthermore, we pointed out the crucial role that education could play in fostering critical awareness of and active participation in citizenship.

Considerations of commonalities and divergences within a society bring us to an inevitable consideration of social cohesion, introduced in the previous section in relation to which languages are, or should be, taught/learned and why. Jansen,

Chioncel and Dekkers (2006: 190) argue that social cohesion concerns a desire to establish balance between the liberty enjoyed by an individual on one hand, and on the other how a society containing these individuals is formed and functions. They argue that beliefs about social cohesion, and how it may be achieved, have shifted from a focus on commonalities to emphasis on 'coping with diversity and dissensus' (Jansen, Chioncel and Dekkers 2006: 191), which supports our stance outlined above. They explain: 'The abstracted nature of shared values and identities covers up inherent diversity, opposition, and inequality, while the defensive attitude to the world "out there" with its "deviant" options and inhabitants easily excludes and divides' (Jansen, Chioncel and Dekkers 2006: 195).

The distinction made between an understanding of social cohesion based on commonalities versus one based on engagement with diversity necessarily has implications for understanding citizenship. Traditionally, the concept of citizenship emerged as one where equality of people in a society was achieved through homogeneity (for example linguistic), and 'difference [meant] inequality' (Lo Bianco 2010: 29). However, Jansen, Chioncel and Dekkers (2006) explain that processes of globalisation challenge a somewhat fixed idea of citizenship and who is a 'legitimate' citizen in the context of a given nation state. Increased movement of peoples, and the engagement of both individuals and communities with multiple others, means that citizenship itself has become more of a fluid concept that may be defined and embodied in a range of different ways. A recent discussion in the *TES* (*Times Educational Supplement*) publication on the nature of citizenship, and citizenship education in the context of UK schools, presented a particularly interesting stance. One head teacher interviewed stated that:

> Citizenship is about connecting citizens to their democracy and their society. Well taught, it should give children a clear view of their own identity in the context of their own culture as well as enable them to *move confidently between cultures*. (Lumby 2017: 45; emphasis added)

This view from a head teacher very much in favour of the potential benefits of citizenship education indicates the importance of developing an understanding of one's own identity before being able to move on to understand others' as well. However, what is noteworthy in this view is how citizenship education could enable one to *transcend cultures* (and perhaps, by extension, identities) through firstly knowing one's own. Such examples of the possibility for fluidity and dynamism in terms of cultural identity/ies, and how they may be explored through the vehicle of citizenship education, move far beyond fears of multiplicity, and the 'other', embodied in the quote above from Jansen, Chioncel and Dekkers. We return to these themes later in this chapter.

Despite our belief that education is likely pivotal in developing active citizenship, it should be pointed out that there are issues with how citizenship is explored through education infrastructures in different contexts around the world. Tonge, Mycock and Jeffery (2012) provide an in-depth discussion of the implementation of citizenship education in the English school system, and reflect on its potential to impact upon civic engagement. They claim that increasing elements of what we have referred to above as shared values were a reaction to instances of civil unrest and examples of the absence of community cohesion across the country (Tonge, Mycock and Jeffery 2012: 582). The stances taken by Labour politicians involved with this implementation of citizenship education in the early 2000s, which centred on 'Britishness' and 'a duty to integrate', are not discordant with more recent moves from a Conservative administration to incorporate 'core British values' into the education system (see the Department for Education document entitled 'Promoting fundamental British values as part of SMSC[1] in schools', from November 2014, for more detail). Tonge, Mycock and Jeffery (2012: 584) present arguments supporting the idea that to take such an approach to citizenship education does little to facilitate social cohesion, and in fact has the possibility of even being damaging in this vein. While we acknowledge the importance of having as a starting point an awareness of what it might mean to be English/British/any other sort of identity linked to a nation state, we are not claiming that raising such awareness should be tantamount to indoctrination. Rather, we are saying this is a foundation upon which individuals are able to compare and contrast other cultures/norms/values/languages, in order to establish an awareness, tolerance and appreciation for those others, as well as close engagement with them. Similarly, Tonge, Mycock and Jeffery (2012: 583) discuss the processes by which the role of diversity, and multiple British identities, was critically examined in the context of citizenship education in England, for example a report on '[promoting] critical thinking about ethnicity, religion and race through an explicit link to political issues and values' (ibid.). Prior to this, Shukra et al. (2004) explored the extent to which social policy in the New Labour era in the United Kingdom established social cohesion as 'progressive' – that is to say, defined and worked at by communities themselves in a way that is appropriate and meaningful to them – or whether social cohesion was more about 'assimilation', that is to say, everyone working towards a top-down definition of what 'Britishness' is decreed to mean.

In preceding sections, we have sought to raise awareness of foundational principles as they relate to language education and citizenship education and have interwoven principles of multilingualism and multiculturalism throughout. We move on now to consider the extent to which there are parallels in the implementation of education for citizenship on one hand and language on the other: what links may be drawn between the two?

## CITIZENSHIP EDUCATION AND LANGUAGE EDUCATION – ESTABLISHING PARALLELS?

We start this discussion by considering the extent to which potential problems with citizenship education (e.g. Tonge, Mycock and Jeffery 2012) may offer interesting parallels with language education. For example, the Global Englishes paradigm (e.g. Galloway and Rose 2015) within the field of applied linguistics has raised the question of *which* language variety, belonging to *whom*, should be taught in a language classroom, and related to this which culture, belonging to whom, should be incorporated into the language classroom (see Hennebry 2013: 139). When it comes to citizenship education, it could similarly be asked *which* citizenship paradigm should be taught, and to *whom* does it belong. Also in parallel with common themes relating to language education, when it has been discussed that the language learned in a classroom should effectively prepare individuals to communicate in 'real world' settings beyond that formal learning environment (Hennebry 2013: 144), it has been argued that there should be a strong connection between the themes raised within formal citizenship education and how citizenship is experienced outside the classroom. Furthermore, it is likely impossible to learn everything you need to be able to speak a language competently and confidently only within the classroom, and so too for citizenship – it is not only learning about it in a formal setting that provides sufficient knowledge and understanding, but actually going outside the classroom to experience it and enact it (Gray and Griffin 2014: 310).

Sigauke (2012) also recognises the relationship between the wider social world outside the classroom, and the citizenship learning that takes place within, arguing that broader ideological forces at play in a given society inevitably shape the kind of citizenship education that takes place within formal education structures (much as Tonge, Mycock and Jeffery 2012, argued was the case in England). With reference to Zimbabwe, Sigauke posits that citizenship education has perhaps been designed and implemented with a view to 'silencing' young people, discouraging critical reflection on issues of ideology and power within that society, and, finally, that such a programme has been designed without due care for young people's own experiences of and beliefs regarding citizenship – again, a top-down rather than a bottom-up approach. Interestingly, similar criticisms are still levelled at citizenship education by some in the British context, arguing that its aim is to encourage people to fall in line, rather than dissent (Lumby 2017: 45). Also in Britain, Shukra et al. (2004: 192) have emphasised the importance of acknowledging valuable bottom-up approaches to engage with diversity that citizens establish for themselves, for example community-based youth work activities which seek to foster a capacity for critical reflection on issues of race and diversity, which they argue politicians are perhaps not always aware of when expressing concerns about diversity in society and social cohesion. Furthermore, Sigauke's discussion of citizenship education requiring performances of fixed ideas of what it means to be a 'good' or a 'bad' citizen similarly invokes doctrines of the 'good' and 'bad' language learner within applied linguistics – for learners in any subject area feeling the need to conform to, and perform, such ideas of 'good' and 'bad' can exert a substantial negative effect on the learning process, and attitudes towards it. It may be all the more worrisome, Sigauke (2012: 222) argues, in contexts where constructions of the 'good' and 'bad' citizen can be highly sensitive, and politically charged.

There are indeed many parallels to be drawn between points that Jansen, Chioncel and Dekkers (2006) make about citizenship education, and language education. For example, they claim that one benefit of citizenship education is making the unfamiliar more comfortable and known – certainly, the same can be said of foreign language learning. They also outline the ways in which citizenship education can play a powerful role in encouraging critical reflection on assumptions made about the seemingly unproblematic relationship between oneself and other 'people and places'. Better understanding and appreciating the inevitable complexity in this regard is, similarly, an aim often achieved through foreign language learning. Finally, they take the stance that non-formal citizenship education – that is to say, learning that takes place through engagement with 'tangible social practices', outside a fixed, formal curriculum – makes an essential contribution to long-term 'active citizenship' (Jansen, Chioncel and Dekkers 2006: 201). They argue that, despite emphasis placed on more formalised approaches to citizenship among those in the political and academic spheres, a formal approach should only be present to supplement and enhance informal citizenship education opportunities. Once more, there are parallels with discussions that take place regarding language learning about the relative value of informal versus formal learning practices: traditionally, a common belief was held that formal learning could provide a foundation of abstract knowledge that could then be applied and developed in more informal learning contexts, that is to say putting the language into use in a target language setting, where communicative competency would be able to develop. (We acknowledge nonetheless that this distinction between what can be achieved in formal and informal learning environments is perhaps less clear-cut nowadays with much more of a focus on communicative approaches even within formal learning contexts; however, that there is indeed a debate about what may be achieved in different learning settings is what we wish to impress.)

In order to frame the discussion of the relationships between citizenship, multilingualism and multiculturalism, it is worth considering how this construct of 'multiple' has so often been equated to 'problematic', the implication then being that 'singular' is equated to 'straightforward'. Linked to the discussion above, about the UK government's promotion of citizenship education as a way of working towards social cohesion, Gray and Griffin (2014: 302) say that governmental support for the construction of a 'citizenship identity' has often been a way to enact social cohesion, by overlooking any manifestation of diversity.

In Isin's (2009) critique of common beliefs about and definitions of citizenship, he raises this point about there often being something of an uncertainty about the notion of 'multiple': 'The unnamed [multinational] figure is unsettling because it belies the modern figure of the citizen with singular loyalty, identity and belonging' (Isin 2009: 368). This echoes Blackledge (2004: 70), who has also raised this point about multilingual individuals lacking a strong, undivided sense of devotion to their nation, which ultimately poses a danger to social cohesion; he argues that immigrants often face expectations from those in their adopted country to shed 'whatever traits make them more different', in favour of appropriating those that cohere with the majority norms, and one core example of such a 'trait' is of course linguistic competence (Blackledge 2004: 73):

> When the dominant majority insists that the ideal model of society or nation is monolingual, we immediately encounter questions about identity and group

> membership (Blommaert & Verschueren, 1998a). If the majority language is endowed with a symbolic status which asserts its superiority over minority languages, there are issues of social justice, as linguistic minority speakers may be excluded from access to, or membership in, the more powerful group. (Blackledge 2004: 68)

In the way that this argument has been put forward for multilingualism, Vermeulen (2004) contends that the principle holds for the notion of multiculturalism also. In his discussion of immigration into the Netherlands, and immigrants seeking citizenship of this nation, he proposes that: 'The centrality of the concept of "integration" in public discourse on multiculturalism represents the dominant view assuming cultural differences to be highly problematic and favoring instead a politics of monoculturalism (Ingleby, 2000)' (Vermeulen 2004: 1).

More recent work by Horner (2015: 214) also supports this idea that for many European countries, integration actually means smoothing over any differences that may arise between different groups in a society as a result of immigration, with the onus being on immigrants themselves to fit in with the norms and expectations of the new country, rather than there being any perception of a responsibility on the part of other citizens of a nation to do so. In a similar vein, but from a more linguistic perspective, a classroom intervention study by Kubota (2001) in the United States sought to address the issue of native English speakers believing that the burden of clarity of communication rests with those categorised as non-native English-speakers, rather than native speakers themselves. Again, the onus is on the 'outsiders' to accommodate to the 'in group', rather than there being a shared responsibility among different sides.

While at the level of the nation state it appears that official doctrines prefer singularity (i.e. monolingualism and monoculturalism), the supra-national level of the European Union actually stands in contrast to this. As Horner (2015: 213) states, 'linguistic diversity is cast as a contemporary goal of the EU', and goes on to point out that this jars somewhat with the deep-rooted 'one nation, one language' ideology present in many countries. Hennebry's (2014: 243) outlining of the relationship between citizenship and language teaching also takes the stance that multilingualism is very much supported at the supra-national European level, indeed as a way of promoting engagement with the notion of European identity and citizenship.

If it is indeed the case that avid engagement with language learning has a role to play in fostering feelings of identity and citizenship at the European level (the implication being that both identity and citizenship can manifest, and be explored, at multiple rather than simply singular levels), it is therefore interesting to consider the possibility of there being some relationship perhaps between the much discussed decline of language learning uptake in the United Kingdom, and the country's decision to leave the European Union in the referendum of June 2016. It could be fruitful to examine the extent to which a broad disregard for language learning at a societal level (see for example Coleman, Galaczi and Astruc 2007; Lanvers 2011) is related to a greater focus on identity and citizenship at the national level,[2] rather than individuals exploring possibilities for multiple identities and senses of citizenship being realised in a more supra-national sphere. Certainly, in the lead-up to the referendum, and following it, there was discussion in the media about the extent to which a vote to leave the European Union would be detrimental to the already tenuous position of languages in Britain (e.g. 'Hold your tongues: why language learners fear a vote for Brexit', which appeared in *The Guardian* newspaper in the days prior to the referendum (Griffin 2016)). Interestingly, however, there were initial indications that in the wake of the Brexit vote there was some increased in interest language learning (e.g. 'Brexit leads to surge in Brits wanting to learn new language, data finds', which appeared in *The Independent* newspaper in May 2017 (Sulleyman 2017)). This provides some suggestion at least that there are individuals in Britain who do not align themselves with the idea of the country being monolingual (as it is so often portrayed, despite the multilingual and multicultural reality – see Lanvers, Hultgren and Gayton (2016: 3) on this 'paradox'), and indeed, could be seeking to hold on to a sense of European citizenship through this practice, one which some feel is perhaps in danger of being eroded, given current political events. A recent example of an impassioned discussion of this issue appeared in *The Guardian* newspaper in October 2016 ('I'm being stripped of my citizenship – along with 65 million others' (Shariatmadari 2016)). This media piece upholds the idea, underpinning this section, that multiple realisations of both citizenship and identity can prove extremely positive.

## CITIZENSHIP AND LANGUAGE – SOME CONCLUDING THOUGHTS

In Chapter 1 we raised the role that education has to play in developing active citizenship and mentioned briefly the possibility of the subject area of languages, and indeed the language teacher specifically, as being central to this process. Elsewhere, Hennebry (2013: 136) has argued that, given the pivotal role played by language in communication, cultural transmission and social cohesion, the practice of foreign language learning is therefore in a privileged position to enable individuals to transcend the boundaries of their own linguistic/cultural/social norms, to develop a far more nuanced and multifaceted perspective in these domains. From the discussion above, it would seem that it is all the more important for such processes to take place in national contexts where there is a pervasive belief about multilingualism and multiculturalism necessarily being divisive, in order to provide, through foreign language learning, an alternative perspective on this. This links with Oates (2007), who reports on how citizenship issues underpin the entire curriculum in the Scottish education context, rather than their simply being discussed in relation to foreign language learning (but does nonetheless claim that foreign language learning is a fundamental space within which citizenship education should be located). She claims that the following questions are ones that may be raised when considering the nexus of citizenship and languages:

Is it possible for monolingual citizens to feel part of a community where several languages may be spoken?

How can we actively participate in our community, global or local, with only one language?

How can we respect and value other cultures, and our own, if we don't know anything about them?

How can we understand each other if we only speak one language? (Oates 2007: 2)

The issues of multilingualism and citizenship lead us finally to a consideration of people who leave their home country to settle in another, and to the questions of language learning and competencies that arise. Is it problematic to simply state that anyone settling in a new country should automatically be required to learn that language? Can one participate fully in a society as an active citizen without doing so? The answers to these questions are far from straightforward.

Perhaps a useful starting point is to go back to the top-down/bottom-up distinction. In many countries, including the United Kingdom, both sufficient linguistic and cultural knowledge needs to be demonstrated through formalised testing in order for one to become a citizen of that country. Again, there are parallels when comparing and contrasting the language and citizenship domains: citizenship tests have been widely criticised, in that they require certain individuals (that is to say, those who have immigrated and wish to become a citizen) to formally demonstrate knowledge of what has been deemed to be the 'culture' of that country (as well as the question of who has decided that the elements presented in the test represent that nation's culture, and the difficulty of pinning down in a formal assessment what is essentially an ever-changing and multifaceted construct), whereas others who happen to have been born in that country do not face the same process. At no point does a citizen by birth have to prove their Britishness (for example) in the way someone born elsewhere, now seeking to become a citizen, has to. The same can be true of language as well: both in the context of citizenship, and elsewhere, it is often the case that non-native speakers are required to prove their linguistic competence in their second language (often English) in a way that native speakers rarely, or ever, have to. Such processes create inequality among individuals; a belief in and support of lesser privileged individuals (by dint of their mother tongue, or of their birthplace) being required to demonstrate their linguistic or cultural skills establishes something of a 'two-tiered' hierarchy of both individuals and communities within a society. To refer back to the notion of translanguaging, it is possible that viewing language competence and use through this framework would strongly bring into question the role of such formalised testing, and again parallels the fluidity in conceptualisations of citizenship as well.

Above, we also raised the question of active citizenship through language – it would be difficult to argue against the idea of competency in the language (or languages) of one's new country facilitating participation in that society. However, our stance is that it is important to enable immigrant individuals and communities to access language learning when necessary, in a way that is appropriate and suitable for them to do so, for them to work towards increasingly meaningful societal participation through their developing linguistic competency. This more bottom-up approach stands in contrast to linguistic competency being a formal, top-down requirement from a country's government. For immigrants in the United Kingdom, for example, developing English language skills should be for the sake of their engagement with the society, rather than it being for the sake of achieving the type of social cohesion defined by its focus on commonalities (as outlined earlier in this chapter). This distinction is elucidated by Cheong et al. (2007: 27) in their discussion of a move in focus and funding away from the support of community languages to English language learning, 'in a bid to promote the learning of a "common" language, and supposedly "core" values and culture among newer immigrants'. As a final point, then, we argue that to focus on the process of English language learning, without appreciating the valuable resources that immigrants possess in terms of competence in other language(s), is to make a detrimental oversight. Framing English (or indeed Welsh or Gaelic in certain parts of the United Kingdom), or whatever the language(s) of the host country may be in any given context, as the one element that matters within an individual's linguistic repertoire can make a person, or a community, and their skills feel devalued or belittled. Furthermore, it can deprive younger generations of the cultural and cognitive benefits of being raised with more than one language, when a message is transmitted that only English should be used in all domains of life. Take, for example, Shukra et al.'s (2004: 193) discussion of the British government's attempts at the time to deal with societal discord (e.g. rioting linked to racial/cultural issues), within which there was the expectation to 'speak English at home'. To return to points raised earlier in this chapter, we align ourselves with other scholars who believe that social cohesion is best achieved through acknowledgement and active engagement with diversity, rather than attempts to avoid it altogether.

**For reflection**

- How is social cohesion understood in your specific context?
- What are your reactions to the parallels drawn between citizenship education and language education? Do they resonate with your own teaching/learning experiences?
- What do you understand to be the strengths and limitations of the different conceptual approaches to bilingualism and multilingualism?
- Do you feel there is a role for citizenship to underpin teaching and learning in higher education?

## NOTES

1. Spiritual, moral, social and cultural development.
2. Here, we are conceptualising British as national, although we are aware that this

is not unproblematic given the different nations that exist within Britain: see Gray and Griffin (2014: 301) for further discussion on this issue. They explain that, in such a context, identity may be conceptualised for an individual at one level, that is to say, a Scottish national identity, while considering themselves simultaneously to be a British citizen.

Chapter 4

# Motivation, language and citizenship

**Objectives**

- To be aware of key theoretical frameworks for language learning motivation.
- To understand the way in which language learning situates the learner in a wider community.
- To critically examine the extent to which the relationship between language learning and citizenship education can be perceived to provide motivational opportunities, both in theory and in teaching practice.

## INTRODUCTION

The rationale for promoting citizenship through foreign language teaching is commonly presented from the perspective that the learning of other languages offers a unique opportunity for developing tolerance and respect for cultural diversity, since it presents a window through which to explore other societies and their ways of life. We have previously considered the ways in which language learning provides a unique context for the development of the values, attitudes and behaviours that might constitute active citizenship. There is also a complementary perspective rooted in the development of language learning motivation, which we have alluded to earlier, and which we will explore in greater detail in this chapter. The relationship between citizenship and language teaching can potentially yield benefits for language learning itself by enriching and promoting language learning motivation, a challenge facing language teachers worldwide, not least those of languages other than English.

Understanding this perspective is valuable because of its potential for winning over the hearts and minds of language teachers who are more likely to take a positive view of any proposals for closer integration of the two subjects if they can see this as a mutually beneficial collaboration (Hennebry 2014). Language teachers and researchers alike have consistently stressed the central role of language learning motivation in promoting language acquisition and attainment. Increased levels of motivation may even allow learners to overcome deficiencies caused by low linguistic aptitude, compensating also for a poor language learning environment (Macaro 2003).

## UNDERSTANDING MOTIVATION

Defining motivation is not a straightforward task and, indeed, MacIntyre (2002) suggests that asking what motivation is may not be a good place to start. Nevertheless, as we proceed to explore frameworks for understanding language learning motivation, it is helpful to have some understanding of what we mean by the term *motivation*. To this end, the definition provided by Williams and Burden (1997) is useful in that it highlights the role of both the cognitive and emotional facets of the learner and the learning process, where other definitions may tend to leave out the latter (MacIntyre 2002). They propose then that motivation is: '. . . a state of cognitive and emotional arousal, which leads to a conscious decision to act and which gives rise to a period of sustained intellectual and/or physical effort in order to attain a previously set goal' (Williams and Burden 1997: 120).

By implication then, in relation to language learning, there needs to be something that provides or stimulates the initial *state of cognitive and emotional arousal*, leading the learner to apply the necessary effort for acting in such a way that will lead to learning. It is here that bringing citizenship education into foreign language teaching can engage learners both cognitively and affectively; cognitively because they are able to see language learning as meaningful and content driven and affectively because they are led towards a view of language learning as offering membership to a wider community and a bridge to other fellow human beings.

## LANGUAGE LEARNING MOTIVATION FRAMEWORKS

There currently exists a range of theoretical frameworks for understanding language learning motivation specifically, many of which integrate a socio-cultural aspect that sees language learning motivation as intrinsically tied to context and society. This chapter focuses on two frameworks in particular that have substantially shaped the field of language learning motivation theory and research: Gardner's socio-educational model and Dörnyei's L2-self system. Gardner's work can be seen to have formed the basis of the L2-self model and indeed has paved the way for much language learning motivation theory today, while the L2-self framework has generated impressive results in terms of explaining language learner motivation.

### Gardner's socio-educational model

Gardner's work originated in the bilingual Canadian context, attempting to understand the language learning motivations of Canadians living across two linguistic communities: French native speaking and English native speaking. In its origins, the socio-educational model proposed that aptitude and motivation were the two main predictive factors for L2 performance. Since Gardner was interested in how language acquisition was possible even where aptitude was below average, he focused on motivation as an explanatory variable. Significantly, Gardner's model proposed that motivational factors originate from and play out in two primary contexts, the formal educational context and the informal cultural context. Each of these contexts within the model was argued to play a distinct role in promoting learner performance, with the educational context being the site of explicit instruction and correction and the cultural context being the area wherein learners become immersed in the target culture and learn implicitly. The social and cultural aspects of the L2 are seen to be a source of motivation for the learner who wishes to become a valued member of the target language community.

Gardner's (1985) model identified a range of components interacting to provide the conditions for language learning motivation. Of these, the two principal components are integrative and instrumental orientations, with integrative seen to have stronger predictive power in terms of ultimate motivation. An integrative orientation refers to 'a sincere and personal interest in the people and culture represented by another language group' (Lambert 1974: 98) – in other words, the learners' interest in the target culture and their desire to be a valued member of the community. Instrumental orientation, on the other hand, refers instead to the learner's beliefs that learning a foreign language can bring about certain pragmatic gains, whether a higher salary or a better job, in short 'the practical value and advantages of learning a new language' (ibid.). These orientations are situated within the learning context, which can be understood both as the social setting and also as the learning situation. In this sense the learner's attitude to the learning situation and their attitude to language learning per se also play a key role in mediating their motivational orientations. As Dörnyei and Ryan (2015) point out, however, recent research has paid closer attention to integrativeness as a stronger explanatory factor for predicting variance in learners' motivation. Such a view of language learning motivation places the social context of foreign language learning centre stage. Furthermore, it implies a view of language learning as a means of real communication and relationship building within society, thus further supporting a stronger educational association between citizenship and foreign language learning. While integrativeness does not in itself constitute motivation, it does give direction to the desire to achieve the goal, to positive attitudes and to the effort that is expended. Together these components constitute motivation for language learning as understood through the socio-educational model (MacIntyre 2002).

The socio-educational model (Gardner and MacIntyre 1993; Gardner 2010) bears particular relevance to our immediate concern, given its focus on the relationship between the learner and the linguistic community. In this model language learning is seen as a means of gaining access to the community and, importantly, the desire to be a *valued* member of the community. The model implies that the learner can be motivated to learn a language by an orientation towards the linguistic community and a desire to contribute meaningfully within that community. Citizenship in its fullest, multicultural and global sense provides a perspective on language learning as more than simply a means of communication but rather as a key to membership in this social group and the enactment of this membership.

Gardner's work in theorising language learning motivation paved the way for much of the progress in the field of language learning motivation today.

Nevertheless, his model has come under criticism in recent decades, leading to the development of new motivational frameworks. One of the key critiques has focused on the concept of integrative motivation. Dörnyei (2009) claims that talk of integrating in the target language community has limited relevance in today's world, given that many learners may never have the opportunity to engage directly with such a community. Indeed, others' easy access to it would also preclude the need for a motivational effort. While there is merit in the critique, perhaps rather than leading us to discard the idea of integration, this might point us to question the way we conceptualise the target language community in a global society. Given the multilingual nature of many societies today, we could argue that the target language community is no longer 'out there' in a place we must travel to, but instead on our doorstep. We could go further and argue that the linguistic community into which the learner may integrate is not one characterised by one given language, but one where multiple languages are spoken and accessed and one in which membership is gained through a multilingual repertoire. This expansion and adaptation of Gardner's original integrative construct strengthens the relationship between language learning and citizenship, as language learning becomes both the linguistic and social means through which learners are able to enact and fulfil their role in the multilingual society they would inhabit.

### Dörnyei's L2 Motivational Self System

The extent to which access and active membership of a linguistic community will be valued by learners relates closely to their self-concept and particularly to the place of linguistic proficiency in their aspirations. In order to better understand this relationship we turn now to the second of our key frameworks known as the L2 Motivational Self System, developed largely by Zoltan Dörnyei.

Based on the premise that the socio-educational model did not sufficiently account for motivation as a psychological trait, recent models have sought to combine knowledge developed in the field of psychology with our understanding about the role of the social context in language learning motivation. The notion of the *self* has generated particular interest within the field of psychology and has in turn enabled the development of language learning motivation theory in a direction that draws together the internal and external worlds of the learner.

In brief, the *selves* framework is based on the idea that individuals are driven to expend sustained effort on a given activity as a means of addressing a discrepancy between their *actual self* and their *ideal* and *future selves*. Among the wide range of self-related issues that have attracted researchers' attention, the *possible selves* and *future self-guides* have been the subject of a distinct subfield of study and are of particular interest to the field of language learning motivation. Self-concept has generally been considered to be the summary of all the self-knowledge related to the way we perceive ourselves in the present and thus the *possible selves* present a new and unique self-dimension referring to a future rather than current self-state. In their seminal paper, Markus and Nurius (1986) distinguished between three types of possible selves: the *ideal* selves that we would wish to become; the selves that we *could* become; and the selves that we *are afraid* of becoming. Our ideal self might refer, for instance, to *our successful self, the loved self, the wise self,* etc., while the feared self might be *the unemployed self, the depressed self, the incompetent self,* and so on. Dörnyei (2009) proposes thinking of the selves as the best case, worst case and default scenarios.

Possible selves are often referred to as *future self-guides*, though as Dörnyei (2009) points out this is more true of the ideal self and the feared self, where the former guides the individual towards the goal and the standards to be reached, and the latter guides away from an undesirable outcome. From a psychological point of view, the ideal self is considered particularly important (Higgins et al. 1994). Building on the work of Markus and Nurius (1986), Higgins proposed the concepts of the ideal self and the ought-to self as future self-guides. This latter concept refers to the representation of the attributes one feels one ought to possess, usually tied to a sense of duty or moral obligations that may in fact be quite distinct from our desires or wishes and therefore quite different to our ideal self. Generally speaking, future self-guides exert a motivational force on the individual who seeks to reduce the discrepancy between their actual self and their ideal or ought-to selves. Applied in the context of language learning, learners' L2 selves act as motivational drivers of the language learning process (Dörnyei and Ushioda 2011).

The socio-educational model together with the possible selves have provided the foundation for the development of the L2 Motivational Self System Model. In essence the L2 self-model does not contradict the existence of the integrative and instrumental orientations nor their significance in motivation theory. Instead it proposes that the learner's future self-guides are key constructs of the L2 motivation system, providing a more complete explanation for the interaction between its various components.

Within the L2 Motivational Self System there are three core components: the *ideal L2 self*; the *ought-to L2 self*; and the *L2 learning experience*. The ideal L2 self is the L2-specific facet of one's 'ideal self', such that if the person we wish to become speaks a second language then the ideal L2 self acts as a guide and powerful motivator for learning that second language. Dörnyei proposes that Gardner's integrative and instrumental motives would belong to this component. The two antecedents of Gardner's integrativeness construct are *attitudes towards members of the L2 community* and *instrumentality*. Dörnyei argues that L2 speakers are the closest parallels to the learner's idealised L2-speaking self. Thus the learner's attitudes to members of the second language community *must* relate to their ideal L2 self-images. He proposes that the more positive our disposition might be towards the L2 speakers, the more attractive the ideal L2 self will be. Drawing on the work of Herbst, Gaertner and Insko (2003), Dörnyei argues that we are attracted to those who emulate the person we wish to be rather than the person we are and that this similarity attraction is driven by the ideal self, thus allowing a reconceptualisation of integrativeness from the perspective of the *selves*. Within a *selves* perspective, instrumentality is understood as bi-directional: promotion and prevention. Instrumentality promotion focuses on attaining the pragmatic gains that come, in this case, from L2 learning, e.g. access to better job opportunities. This particular orientation is seen to relate closely to the ideal L2 self. Preventative instrumentality, on the other hand, refers to a wish to avoid failure or disappointment, e.g. failing exams or disappointing parents. This aspect would constitute part of the ought-to L2 self.

Thus, the L2 Motivational Self System is comprised of the ideal L2 self, the ought-to L2 self and the L2 learning experience. This last component acknowledges the work conducted in the 1990s recognising the impact on motivation of elements such as the classroom environment, the teacher, the curriculum, and so on.

## THE ROLE OF CULTURE

Recent work conducted in East Asian contexts has indicated a need to further investigate the extent to which some of the concepts that constitute the core to language motivation theories may be understood differently depending on cultural context and philosophical heritage. The *self* and *integrativeness* are two such concepts. In a study looking at language motivation among Taiwanese students, the researchers propose a distinct orientation for students from this particular cultural context, extending to other Confucian heritage contexts. They argue that the motivation of participants in their study is better explained by a *required orientation*. This may initially seem rather like Dörnyei's idea of the ought-to self whereby learners seek to meet the expectations of parents or teachers. However, Chen, Warden and Chang (2005) and colleagues suggest that the internalisation of requirements in the Confucian heritage context is such that the construct of the *required orientation* is in fact distinct from the Western understanding of meeting expectations. In other words, while the Western learner may strive to meet expectations that are external to their own aspirations or even identity, parent or teacher expectations will be an integral part of the Confucian heritage learner's identity and will play a significant role in the realisation of that identity. This particular avenue of enquiry is one that needs further exploration and has the potential to yield interesting and significant insights into the nature of the relationship between motivation and cultural context. In terms of the relationship between language teaching and citizenship, the insights yielded by Chen and colleagues only serve to further highlight the potential for collaboration between these two substantive areas. If indeed the requirements of significant others such as teachers, parents and society at large are intrinsically associated with learners' language learning motivations, then language becomes a means through which the learner can realise their ought-to self as an internalised dimension of their ideal self.

## INTEGRATIVENESS, INSTRUMENTALISM, FUTURE SELF-GUIDES AND CITIZENSHIP

Whether language learners at all stages of cognitive and psychological development can be said to have a developed L2 self is a question worthy of research, not least since this would have important implications in terms of the amount of time and pedagogical resources that language teachers might expend on promoting such a self among their learners. The foreign language teacher can encourage the development of the ideal L2 selves through engaging learners with the target cultures, promoting values of cultural appreciation and encouraging critical intercultural reflection. In so doing, learners are supported in the development of new identities that incorporate an intercultural dimension and can begin to see themselves as citizens operating beyond their local context. If they can see the ways in which learning the language would allow them to actively participate in such communities, thus gaining legitimacy as group members, then this can constitute an important motivation for language learning, while at the same time promoting positive citizenship values.

At the heart of both Gardner's framework and Dörnyei's L2 models lies the idea that motivated language learners have a desire to connect to the linguistic community and that they wish to relate to its speakers. In light of the theories we have discussed, it is not a huge leap to suggest that if a learner's ideal self is an active citizen in a context that can be more readily accessed through proficiency in an L2, then this too can act as a motivator, bringing citizenship and foreign language learning into a symbiotic relationship. The sum of the key theories in language learning motivation can be said to lead us to the understanding that language learning motivation is likely to have a unique advantage from the point of view of linguistic development seen as contributing to social and personal development and, where possible, as playing a part in a broadening linguistic community. This can only be the case, however, if the learner understands the community and sees the language they are learning as integral to the identity of its speakers and thus as more than a system of syntactic and lexical rules: 'language is not conceived of as a neutral medium of communication, but is understood with reference to its social meaning' (Norton 2013: 45).

The work of Gardner and that of Dörnyei has highlighted the significance also of instrumental orientations in language learning. Much of the problem teachers face today lies in convincing language learners that language learning will be useful for real purposes that are meaningful to them. To a large degree this is due to the fact that learners do not necessarily envisage foreign language use as a part of their daily lives. This can apply to learners of languages other than English, where the predominance of English in the international work context can give a misguided impression that English is the only language necessary. However, it can apply also in the case of learners learning English in contexts where the pragmatic value may not be immediately evident; this is perhaps particularly true of rural settings more shielded from the impacts of internationalisation and globalisation.

Language teaching that promotes an instrumental orientation would seek to expose learners to the opportunities that exist both in their own home context and beyond for those with linguistic skills. Nevertheless, there is a danger in adopting a purely instrumentalist view of language that divorces language from its speakers, their culture and their identity. Those whose work requires them to interact with speakers of languages other than their own need also to have cultural sensitivity, as well as an openness to new experiences and to diverse ways of life. Possessing only the linguistic tools without such attitudes and perspectives has little to do with developing citizens who are able to engage meaningfully in today's multicultural society. Thus, integrativeness becomes the context in which teachers might also develop an awareness of the instrumental value of language learning. Indeed, existing research supports the idea that learners are attracted to both the integrative and instrumental benefits of language learning. Working with secondary school learners in Rome, Creanza (1997) found that the students cited prospects of employment, cultural enrichment and overseas travel, as well as integrative factors relating to the kind of ideal selves the learners envisioned as their key motivations for foreign language learning. Meanwhile, Hennebry (2011) reported that adolescent foreign language learners across European countries valued the mobility foreign language learning offers across local, national and supra-national spheres, for socialising as well as working in other cultural contexts.

The development of citizenship through foreign language teaching can be seen to tap into particular motivational factors; developing students' understandings of other national, ethnic and cultural identities and enabling them to value and respect differences has the potential to raise their desire to acquire the necessary linguistic tools that will enable communication and dialogue with those of other identities. In turn, foreign language teaching that succeeds in equipping learners with the tools with which to participate in social and political processes and in the shaping of society would arguably make a unique contribution to promoting and enabling active citizenship beyond national frontiers wherein the learner may be required to speak a language other than their mother tongue. Furthermore, the interplay between citizenship studies and foreign language learning offers support for adopting a CLIL-based (Content and Language Integrated Learning-based) approach. This involves teaching a curricular subject through the medium of a language other than that normally used.

One of the characteristics that differentiates foreign language teaching from other curriculum subjects is that the content of the instruction is to some extent also the medium of instruction; arguably a rather limited perspective on foreign language learning that presents the learning of vocabulary and grammar as an end in itself rather than as a means to the expression of meaningful dialogue that facilitates participation in society at cognitive levels matching the stage of the learner. Starkey (2002) argues that the current state of foreign language teaching in the United Kingdom, for instance, 'infantilises' the learner; while learners engage with critical discussion of social and political systems and structures within the citizenship class, they go little beyond describing their pets in the foreign language class. The calls for the development of citizenship within foreign language teaching require an overhaul of the foreign language curriculum that has not yet taken place but that if undertaken could result in greater motivational potential for foreign language learning as well as a vehicle for learners to see themselves as international and cosmopolitan citizens with the necessary knowledge and understanding to play a part in social processes. Indeed, the promotion of active citizenship rests to a large degree on developing intercultural communication and a sense of belonging to a community (integrative motivation) on the one hand and, on the other hand, on citizens participating in social and political processes (instrumental motivation).

This chapter explores key theoretical models for understanding motivation for language learning. It identifies core constructs seen to play an important role in shaping and directing language learning motivation and in doing so highlights the symbiotic relationship between citizenship development and the enhancement of language learning motivation. It proposes that a closer integration of citizenship and language learning can provide a clearer purpose for language learning.

**For reflection**

- In the context of the motivation theories you have read about in this chapter, how might learners' experience of language learning vary depending on the integration or exclusion of the intercultural dimension of language learning? Can you think of any examples that might illustrate this?
- For many teachers, integrating an intercultural dimension to their language teaching seems desirable but unrealistic given the curriculum's time constraints and assessment demands. At the same time, language teachers around the world struggle to motivate their learners. To what extent and in what way do you think integrating an intercultural dimension, meeting curriculum and assessment demands and motivating learners may be interconnected?

Chapter 5

# Language and citizenship in the curriculum

**Objectives**

- To examine existing curricula in the context of citizenship education.
- To critically consider the extent to which the relationship between language and citizenship education promoted in the literature is seen to translate into curriculum frameworks.
- To critically analyse the relationship between theory, policy and practice in the context of language and citizenship education.

## INTRODUCTION

The curriculum and its associated assessment structures are a key means through which education policy filters down to the classroom. Thus, future citizens are socialised at a fundamental level through classroom delivery of the curriculum. Furthermore, the place and status accorded to citizenship in the curriculum and its delivery in the classroom is one indication of a commitment on the part of the state and educators alike to equip young people for full social participation, promoting skills of critical reflection and developing an understanding of their role within the local and global community, in order to be able to contribute meaningfully to social cohesion, whether through informal fostering of intercultural communication or through more formal participation in social enterprises.

In light of the claims in a range of policy documents related to the important role of language learning in preparing citizens for participation in today's multilingual and multicultural contexts, this chapter would like to critically consider the language curricula across contexts, examining the relative opportunities and challenges presented for promoting the relationship between language learning and citizenship education.

Citizenship development in the curriculum can typically take the form of skills development for the practice of active citizenship or that of addressing the required knowledge to facilitate and enable civic participation. Language learning has a part to play in both these areas, developing intercultural communication skills for building bridges to other cultural groups and providing understanding of the cultural groups learners reach out to, through interaction but also through exploration of historical events, ways of life and belief systems that shape cultural groups. Recalling the discussion in Chapter 3, language teaching for citizenship education might usefully combine the teaching of 'high culture' and 'culture as a social practice' allowing learners to both understand how cultures evolve and develop key competencies for intercultural citizenship (Byram 1998). Discussions around intercultural citizenship and intercultural communicative competence in recent years have seen a focus on skills development (procedural knowledge), with little focus on declarative knowledge. Yet, an accurate critical reflection, a concept at the heart of any effective intercultural communicative competence, is contingent on having a deep understanding and comprehension of the subject matter, thus it presupposes some sort of thorough knowledge of that on which to critically reflect (Willingham 2007). Avoiding essentialism is not an argument that can justify avoiding the material productions of a given culture or denying the existence of a different other by divorcing language from culture, but instead it means simultaneously promoting skills of self-reflection, opening to curiosity and to the other, and encouraging appreciation and enjoyment of diversity as a richness of society while developing an understanding of the ways in which those of other cultural groups define themselves, both individually and collectively.

## CURRICULUM ORIENTATIONS

Surveying the development of integrated multilingual curricula, Meier (2014) provides a useful framework for understanding the orientations that underpin language curricula and associated documents. Her analysis considered proposals for multilingual curricula across Switzerland, Luxembourg, Belgium and the United States and identified ten key orientations framing the direction and conceptualisation of language learning, namely: language learning orientation; competence orientation; learner orientation; language awareness; content orientation; intercultural orientation; collaborative orientation; action orientation; evaluation orientation; and local orientation. While all these orientations are integral to language teaching, the present discussion focuses on the intercultural and the action orientations, as these seem particularly pertinent to the integration of citizenship in language teaching.

Meier's (2014) documentary analysis identified a number of features of the intercultural orientation built into the curricula and syllabi. Firstly, it highlighted a strong emphasis on intercultural competence and understanding across contexts (Kleppin 2004; Candelier 2008; Coyle, Holmes and King 2009; Hufiesen 2011). The analysis also revealed three dimensions of the cultural component: recognising cultural communalities; gaining awareness of the target language speaking culture; comparison of the target culture with the learner's own culture. How this translates into practice is a crucial question, but the inclusion of an intercultural dimension offers the potential to build towards the active practice of cosmopolitan citizenship, providing a context for promoting independence from a single linguistic and conceptual system (Liddicoat 2005) and exposing learners to new worldviews for decentering and understanding the perspectives of others (Kramsch 1993).

## ACTION ORIENTATION

The action orientation, which Meier (2014) observes, has been a part of the Common European Framework of Reference for Languages, since 2001. This orientation conceives language learners as social agents, with a social contribution to make. It reflects also an experiential view of learning (Kolb 1984) where knowledge is created through the transformation of experience (Kolb 1999: 2), from concrete experience, to abstract conceptualisation, reflective observation and active experimentation. Liddicoat (2014) argues that intercultural perception is not simply a manifestation of awareness or knowledge, but also entails action. During the process of language use in dialogue entailing interpretation and expression of meaning across cultural boundaries, learners draw on awareness and knowledge gained through previous experience and learn to recognise that messages can be interpreted in multiple ways and that meaning is many times culturally embedded (Liddicoat and Scarino 2010). The action orientation of language curricula offers the opportunity for generating such experiences, emphasising the practice of language in real situations. For this reason learning should take place both inside and outside the school, whether through community-based projects, field trips, voluntary work or internships (García 2009). The work of Meier and Daniels (2013) indicates that experiential learning that has a focus on contributing to the community wherein language learning takes place is associated with effective language learning, social integration and student satisfaction.

The action orientation of language teaching can be enacted through classroom-based opportunities for discussion of and reflection on one's own cultural identity and that of others within the context of simulated intercultural encounters, but such opportunities may be more limited than direct encounters in their potential for learners' self-discovery and the revelation of deep-seated assumptions and attitudes. Furthermore, opportunities to engage with and contribute to society as part of the learning process resonate with the critical paradigm focusing on social change and social justice (García and Sylvan 2011), while Coyle, Holmes and King (2009) also find echoes with the aim of social integration and social cohesion, both of which are core aims of language learning and citizenship education. The action orientation aligns closely with the idea that language learning can and should provide a means for positive social action, promoting active civic participation and enabling learners to contribute meaningfully to society.

## INTERCULTURAL ORIENTATION

Decentering and the ability to value other perspectives as valid and meaningful is the result of deliberate and explicit teaching that engages learners with critical examination of the assumptions they bring to intercultural encounters and promotes skills and knowledge for understanding and interpreting such experiences; being interculturally aware involves a continuous process of intercultural learning through experience and critical reflection (Liddicoat 2014). There is no end point at which we finally achieve an intercultural state, because being positively intercultural is an ongoing work of action in response to new experiences and of reflection on this action. Thus, a key implication for curriculum development is the need for a dual focus on process as well as product. Intercultural appreciation as part of citizenship practice requires an ongoing commitment, an openness to input that transforms the way we see the world and a willingness to examine and re-examine our attitudes and reactions to diversity, not necessarily adopting new points of view as much as understanding the other's right to diversity, to also be a self. As others before him, Liddicoat (2014) proposes that culture is not about *information and things*, but rather about *actions and understanding* (p. 838). Yet, actions and understanding need to be based on knowledge; understanding the present begins by knowing about the past. Present-day individuals may not be understood in their unique totality by examining their collective history, but neither can they be completely divorced from this past. The history, literature and artworks of a culture are important representations through which social groups express their beliefs, values and identity. Perhaps then, language teaching for intercultural citizenship does not require exclusion of information and things, but rather a different approach to them. Rather than being the object of study themselves, they become a means for deeper reflection and for promoting understanding of the self and others. It is through engagement with literary texts, for instance, that the learner explores differences between their own culture and that of the target culture (Kramsch and Nolden 1994). This requires a pedagogical focus not only on the product of learning, but also on the process.

## CURRICULUM FOR INTERCULTURAL CITIZENSHIP

Language curricula with a citizenship orientation would engage learners in an exploration of the cultural practices of the target language community, as well as examining the socio-historical contexts in and through which these practices have been shaped. They should provide opportunities for learners to directly experience the target culture. This can be through first-hand interaction with members of the target community, but also, for instance, through multimedia, integration of authentic materials, and/or exposure to both classical and present-day literary texts from both well-known and lesser-known writers. Closely tied to such exposure, the curriculum should offer space and structures for learners to engage in a dialogue that uncovers their assumptions, experiences of and attitudes towards other cultures, the assumptions they hold regarding their own and other cultures, and the sources of and influences on these perceptions and attitudes. Learners should be encouraged to reflect on the ways their intercultural experiences impact on their attitudes and assumptions, considering also what this process teaches them about the nature of intercultural interactions. Building these key principles into a framework for pedagogy, Liddicoat et al. (2003) propose five key principles of intercultural pedagogy helpful for developing language curricula for active cosmopolitan citizenship:

1. *Active construction:* learning is viewed as purposeful, active engagement in a process of meaning interpretation and meaning making in interaction with others, accompanied by a continuous process of reflection in variable contexts on one's self and others.
2. *Making connections:* connections are made between existing perceptions and new conceptions and between previous and new experiences. In challenging previous knowledge, new insights are generated, in light of which students connect, reorganise, elaborate and extend their understanding.
3. *Interaction:* learning and communication are social and interactive. Interacting and communicating interculturally means continuously developing one's own understanding of the relationship between one's own language and culture framework and that of others.
4. *Reflection:* learning involves becoming aware of how individuals think, know and learn about language, culture, knowing, understanding and the relationship between these, as well as concepts such as diversity, identity, experiences and one's own intercultural thoughts and feelings.
5. *Responsibility:* learning depends on learners' attitudes, dispositions and values, developed over time.

These principles outline a constructivist framework for intercultural learning where the skills and attitudes necessary for cosmopolitan citizenship can be developed. Scarino and Liddicoat (2009) proposed that these principles should constitute a framework to guide pedagogical decisions. That practice was conceived as a series of four interrelated processes of noticing, comparing, reflecting and interacting. In the noticing stage, learners become aware of similarities and differences between their own culture and others, and between their perceptions and the input they receive, making meaning from intercultural experiences. Crozet and Liddicoat (2000) suggest that noticing is not a naturally occurring process in the language classroom, rather opportunities come as result of deliberate curriculum planning. The comparison stage engages learners with a process of comparison, identifying similarities and differences as a source for reflection, itself a core component of active intercultural citizenship (Kohonen 2000). The reflection stage requires learners to interpret, to understand and to make personal sense of their intercultural experience; while the final interaction stage actively engages the learner with diversity through direct experience, providing opportunities to create personal meaning, to communicate those meanings and to explore and reshape them in response to others.

Throughout the process learners also reflect on their role within intercultural interactions and how their language use, perceptions and assumptions contribute to the unfolding nature of those interactions. Learners begin to see themselves as active intercultural social agents able to use language meaningfully, to generate real consequences and bring about social cohesion.

Social cohesion is either strengthened or weakened through this intercultural dialogue and learners can be guided to reflect on the ways in which they shape dialogue through the content and language of the messages they convey.

## CURRICULUM CASES

In light of the above discussion, we now consider language curricula in France, Ireland, Spain, England and Finland, exploring the ways in which they promote knowledge, skills and attitudes for the practice of citizenship.

Across the curricula, the general objectives refer to developing cultural awareness and, in some cases, to enabling students to draw comparisons between their own culture and the learning and valuing of diversity. The objectives stated in England's curriculum are somewhat less committed to the idea of intercultural awareness and comprehension, going only so far as to seek to establish some cultural comparisons, an approach that in itself runs the risk of cultural essentialism.

Though the objectives of the examined curricula do not explicitly address citizenship, effective practice of citizenship is contingent on developing corresponding attitudes and understanding. In this sense the objectives set out in the French, Irish, English and Finnish curricula constitute an initial step towards this development by outlining the need for learners to understand cultural differences and similarities, value otherness and distance themselves from ethnocentric attitudes.

**Box 5.1** General objectives of the language teaching curricula in France, Ireland, Spain, England and Finland (own translation)

**General objectives**

***France***

Students should be aware of similarities and differences that exist between their own culture and that of the target country and should learn to be open to changing their perspective of each.

***Ireland***

*(Junior cycle)*

– To give pupils an awareness of another culture, and thus a more objective perspective of their own culture.

– To give pupils the possibility of access to sources of information, culture enrichment and entertainment through the target language.

– To encourage and equip pupils to consider participating in social and cultural activities, which may involve some use of the target language.

*(Senior cycle)*

– To foster in learners such communicative skills in the target language as will enable them to:

- extract information and derive enjoyment from the mass media and the more accessible literature of the target language community;
- consider as a realistic option the possibility of pursuing leisure activities, further study and/or career opportunities through the medium of the target language.

– To equip learners with a broad acquaintance with the cultural, social and political complexion of countries in which the target language is a normal medium of communication and thus to help raise their awareness of cultural, social and political diversity generally.

***Spain***
(The general aims here refer to the Common European Framework for language learning but make no reference to culture.)

***England***
The study of languages should include: learning about different countries and cultures; and comparing pupils' own experiences and perspectives with those of people in countries and communities where the target language is spoken.

***Finland***
The tasks of the instruction are to accustom the pupils to using their language skills and educate them in understanding and valuing how people live in other cultures too . . . As an academic subject, a foreign language is a cultural and skill subject.
*In grades 3–6:*
The pupil is to realise that languages and cultures are different, but not different in value.

Explicit reference to the need for critical reflection and opportunities for action would be a useful addition to curriculum objectives, given the significant bearing this has for how language learning is conceived of and which language pedagogies are implemented. This would consolidate the learning experience (Kolb 1984) and enable learners to reflect on how language learning may facilitate and shape their active participation in society within and beyond cultural boundaries (Meier 2014). Through an action orientation, learners can experience language learning as a meaningful endeavour, which facilitates the building of intercultural relationships for social cohesion. This orientation is barely evident in some curriculum objectives, with the notable exception of the Irish curriculum. The junior cycle objectives for Ireland's curriculum for foreign languages are: *To encourage and equip pupils to consider participating in social and cultural activities, which may involve some use of the target language*; while the senior cycle aims: *To foster in learners such communicative skills in the target language as will enable them to consider as a realistic option the possibility of pursuing leisure activities, further study and/or career opportunities through the medium of the target language.* Thus, language learning is framed as a real means of communication, through which learners may more fully participate in society. The role of language teaching here is to equip learners for such participation.

The strongest orientation across the curricula considered here is the intercultural. In the case of France and Spain, references to culture seem primarily to focus on *information and things* (Liddicoat 2014). For instance, in France:

> [During the sixth and fifth years] students learn to tell and describe through the medium of a variety of authentic materials (songs, advertisements, film extracts, stories, poetry, sayings, etc.)
> [Students] learn about the main historical events and geographical landmarks

and in Spain:

> **Socio-cultural contents**
> Pupils should acquire an awareness of the society and culture of the communities in which the target language is spoken . . .
>
> The following topics will be considered in the language learning process:
> - Daily life (festivals, timetables, etc.)
> - Living conditions (home, work, etc.)
> - Personal relations (social structures and relationships between the members of the linguistic community)
> - Values, beliefs and behaviours (institutions, art, humour, etc.)
> - Body language (gestures, visual contact, etc.)
> - Social conventions (behavioral conventions and taboos)
> - Ritual habits (celebrations, ceremonies, etc.)

Although the topics seem to convey culture as *information and things*, the pedagogies that are used to teach these topics can potentially promote *action and understanding*, through opportunities for discussion, reflection and through the unpacking of prior beliefs. England's framework makes brief reference to intercultural learning in this sense, explicitly emphasising decentring and skills of comparison:

> **Key concepts**
> ***Intercultural understanding***
> (1) appreciating the richness and diversity of other cultures
> (2) recognising that there are different ways of seeing the world, and developing an international outlook

The Finnish curriculum adopts a combined approach, promoting the learning of '*the similarities and differences between that culture and Finnish culture*' and '*the main contents of . . . the culture of their own language and the target language*' but framing such learning in the context of '*the perspective of the language regions of the pupil's language and the language being studied*' and significantly '*learn to communicate with representatives of the target language culture . . . in a manner natural to that culture*'. Thus, the learner is exposed to the cultural content but learns to view this content both from their own and the other perspective, learning also the need to show respect for other cultural forms of expression.

It is interesting to note that the Finnish curriculum is the only one that includes learners learning about their own culture; this is significant in enabling meaningful and rich cultural comparisons and reflections. Furthermore, the Finnish curriculum is the only one to include intercultural learning in its assessment. On the one hand it can be argued that assessing awareness of cultural differences and similarities might imply a static and rigid – rather than dynamic and evolving – view of culture. On the other hand, the move raises the profile of intercultural learning, arguably aligning more closely with the intended goals of language learning.

**Objectives**
*Cultural skills*
The pupil will get to know the culture of the target language and will gain a preliminary introduction to the similarities and differences between that culture and Finnish culture.
Learn to communicate with representatives of the target language culture in everyday situations, in a manner natural to that culture.

*Core contents*
Situations and subject areas from the perspective of the language regions of the pupil's language and the language being studied.
Basic knowledge of one's own culture and the culture of the target language culture in Finland, depending on the language.

**Description of good performance at the end of the sixth grade**
*Cultural skills*
The pupils will know the main contents of, and key similarities and differences between, the culture of their own language and the target language.
Be able to interact with speakers of the target language in simple everyday situations.

Ireland's curriculum is more detailed in its integration of cultural awareness. As with the case of Finland, this curriculum adopts a combined approach, stipulating in some detail the cultural content to be taught, while also engaging learners with critical examination of stereotypes, and reflection on the ways in which cultural differences may result in misunderstandings.

**Cultural Awareness**
***General Activity/Theme: Learning in the target language about the present-day culture associated with the target language***
Performance targets:
– Understanding the main elements of target language material (notably newspaper and magazine articles, listening material and literary texts) on contemporary aspects of target language community life such as the following:

- everyday activities (shopping, getting to work, eating and drinking, etc.)
- customs and traditions
- the arts and entertainment
- the range and role of the mass media.

*General Activity/Theme: Reading modern literary texts (notably novels, short stories, poems and plays, or extracts from these) in the target language*
Performance targets:
– Understanding the main elements of the surface meaning of a modern literary text in the target language.
– Identifying meanings present but not overtly expressed in such a text.
– Appreciating the 'tone' of such a text.

*General Activity/Theme: Describing and discussing everyday life in the target language community*
Performance targets:
– Describing the similarities and contrasts between normal everyday life in Ireland and normal everyday life in one of the communities associated with the target language, with particular reference to, for example:

- where people live; how people are educated; what people work at; how much people earn in various jobs; how much holiday time people have and how they use it; what kinds of amenities people expect to have provided in their cities, towns and villages; what people eat and drink, where and at what times; what kinds of shops are available; what kinds of public services are available; what aspects of the natural environment are prominently referred to in conversation and/or involved in work and leisure activities.

– Discussing the relative advantages and disadvantages of the Irish way of life and that of the target language community in respect of the above areas of experience.
– Identifying differences between Irish and target language community behaviour in everyday circumstances with the potential to occasion misunderstanding, embarrassment or offence.
– Critically examining national stereotypes.

*General Activity/Theme: Understanding, describing and discussing aspects of the relations between the target language community and Ireland*
Performance targets:
– Outlining in broad terms the principal links between the target language community and Ireland (e.g. co-membership of the EU, literary connections, tourism, sport, etc.).
– Stating and defending personal opinions about the desirability of maintaining, developing or changing Ireland's links with the community in question.

*General Activity/Theme: Understanding, describing and discussing in general terms issues that transcend cultural divisions*
Performance targets:
– Discussing issues such as:

- teenager culture; the generation gap; 'entertainment'; environment and ecology; sexual and racial equality; ethnic minorities; health and lifestyle;

changing perspectives regarding human relationships (marriage, the family, etc.); the European dimension; the Third World.
– Describing how such issues present themselves in Ireland and in the target language community.
– Stating and defending personal opinions in respect of such issues.

The curriculum expects learners to understand the benefits of forging relationships between Ireland and other cultures, framing language learning as a tool for intercultural communication and bridge building and for promoting social cohesion. While there is a clear intercultural orientation throughout, in stipulating that learners need to be able to state and defend their position on intercultural relations, as well as social issues such as ethnic minorities, changing perspectives on human relationships, sexual and racial equality, etc., the curriculum is also underpinned by an action orientation. There is a clear assumption that learners will participate in social dialogue on issues of social import, through the target language and in ways that are culturally sensitive.

## CURRICULAR CHALLENGES AND OPPORTUNITIES

The integration of an intercultural orientation is evidence of progress in language curriculum design and reflects the advances that have been made in the way we understand the nature of language and language learning from a theoretical perspective, as well as in terms of the needs and social practices that characterise today's global society. In this sense, the curricula align with Osler and Starkey's (2003) framework for understanding cosmopolitan citizenship, underlining the need to respect diversity, work collaboratively, understand one's own cultural standpoint and promote solidarity and equity at all levels, for the flourishing of the individual and society.

None of the curricula specifically address the legal aspect of citizenship rights or indeed the mechanisms through which citizens can access their rights. While some might argue that it is not the job of language teachers to teach about citizens' rights, as long as theory and policy continue to interrelate foreign language and citizenship reference to citizenship rights and access to those rights is integral to language education for citizenship development. Thus, the issue becomes one of generating a shared understanding of the purposes of language learning that is shared among theorists, policy makers, teachers and learners alike.

The Crick Report (1998) suggested that citizenship education should focus on three key areas: social and moral responsibility; community involvement; and political literacy. It further proposed that language teaching could contribute to citizenship development's aims by offering a contrasting perspective from other countries on national, supra-national and world events, and on issues relating to the form and practice of citizenship. Lawes (2000: 92) argues that while this is a laudable aim, 'it is difficult to see how real justice might be done to such weighty political issues within an already crowded MFL curriculum'.

Underlying concerns about overcrowding in the curriculum are questions about the nature and purposes of such a curriculum. Language teaching needs to equip learners with the necessary linguistic knowledge for effective communication, but Starkey (2002) expresses a concern that in the process of tailoring the curriculum to students' existing proficiency levels there is a risk infantilising the language learner, requiring them to engage with content that is considerably below their cognitive capacities. On the one hand, at policy level, there needs to be close alignment between language curriculum objectives and the linguistic and cognitive resources of learners throughout the learning stages. On the other hand, teachers need to make professional pedagogical decisions about the ways in which they utilise students' existing resources both in L1 and in L2 as tools for adapting the level of cognitive challenge built into the syllabus and classroom tasks. Furthermore, a careful examination of the aims of language curricula would usefully consider what is achievable within the time and resource constraints that most teachers experience.

The idea that learners will develop linguistic competence that enables effective communication is unrealistic in contexts where class time can be as little as one hour a week and class size can be anything from thirty students upwards. If instead the aim is to promote students' intercultural communicative competence and to stimulate their interest in culturally diverse ways of life through exposure to one specific culture and language, then this needs to be reflected in the content and nature of the language curriculum.

Previous literature has identified some of the key features of effective citizenship education. Osler and Starkey (1999), for instance, note that individuals should learn how to seek out relevant information independently, that projects for citizenship development should address information and rights but also identities and feelings, as well as structural inequalities, and that such projects are most successful when they combine opportunities to develop participatory skills.

Meanwhile, Walkington and Wilkins (2000) conducted a study on the effects and outcomes on primary school teachers of a period of teaching abroad. While all teachers delivered the curriculum objectives, those with teaching abroad experience also integrated 'global' citizenship education aims because they saw this as integral to their role as educators. Furthermore, those who had taught abroad adopted a process-oriented, participatory pedagogy developing critical thinking skills and personal growth. Those who had not taught abroad primarily used a transmission-based model of teaching. While the participants in Walkington and Wilkins' (2000) study were geography teachers, language teaching in many contexts is characterised by a transmission approach that fails to provide opportunities for promoting personal growth.

Having identified effective structures and pedagogies for developing citizenship, teachers also need to be equipped and enabled for integrating such approaches in their practice. Walkington and Wilkins (2000) suggest that effective citizenship education starts with appropriate teacher education for participatory teaching styles. Indeed, studies have suggested that while language teachers across the board feel confident to teach learners about other cultures, they are less clear on what it might mean to promote skills for active citizenship and perhaps particularly how to intertwine this with the teaching of language (Hennebry 2014).

The issue of teacher education is discussed in greater detail in Chapter 8, yet it is a central consideration in developing an appropriate curriculum, since curriculum effectiveness depends on adequately equipping teachers for its delivery. While language teachers have both linguistic competence and the direct experience of other cultures and worldviews to take the language learner beyond their national confines, they may have less experience of pedagogies particularly suited to citizenship education.

This chapter provides a critical review of orientations in a range of language curricula in the context of citizenship development. It identifies varying degrees of an intercultural orientation across the curricula. Nevertheless, there is little explicit integration of citizenship either in terms of rights or responsibilities. Given the dissonance between macro policy and curriculum policy, as well as some perceived shortcomings of the teacher education curriculum, this chapter outlines challenges that must be overcome if the aimed-for goal is that of developing language education models that would prepare learners to be active citizens.

**For reflection**

- Consider the language curriculum implemented in your teaching context. To what extent is citizenship development explicitly or implicitly integrated?
- What opportunities does the curriculum present for the development of citizenship, through the topics or skills it focuses on?
- To what extent and in what ways might the integration of citizenship topics promote the intended learner outcomes?

## Chapter 6

# Understanding language learning and citizenship education in context

**Objectives**

- To critically understand the ways in which socio-historical variations, curriculum developments and language attitudes interact with one another.
- To compare and contrast the ways in which the relationship between policy and practice on language and citizenship education is enacted across these two specific contexts (England and Hong Kong).

## INTRODUCTION

Chapter 5 critically examined the existing languages framework implemented in England drawing comparisons with other language curricula existent in other contexts. On the one hand, the framework in England draws on ideas of decentring, cultural comparison, intercultural understanding and appreciation. Yet, the explicit integration of citizenship is largely constrained to the preamble, rather than to the specific content. This chapter examines key policy documents, developing a more detailed understanding of the way language teaching is viewed in relation to citizenship in the context of England. The chapter then considers Hong Kong's English language curriculum, examining the extent to which the socio-cultural and socio-historical differences across the contexts are reflected in the way language teaching is perceived. Each context presents an interesting case; England voted to leave the European Union, representing a shift away from a supra-national, regional union, while Hong Kong is moving towards union, transitioning from British governance, under the banner of 'one country, two systems', maintaining aspects of its socio-political character while responding also to changing political realities.

## ENGLAND

England is viewed on the one hand as a melting pot of cultural diversity and on the other hand as isolationist (Orde 2015; Klaas and Dirsus 2016). For some time, citizenship education in England has recognised the need for a conception of citizenship that embraces cultural diversity as a rich resource of British society (e.g. Ajegbo, Kiwan and Sharma 2007) and in this regard the relationship between language learning and citizenship development has again been emphasised, both for economic and social reasons.

The White Paper,[1] *Excellence in Schools* (Department for Education and Skills 1997), highlighted concerns about the diminishing importance given to citizenship education, and pledged to 'strengthen education for Citizenship and the teaching of democracy in schools'. The formation of the Advisory Group on the Teaching of Citizenship and Democracy in schools, which produced the Crick Report (1998) making recommendations towards a subsequent review of the National Curriculum, was a key step towards this strengthening of education for citizenship. The Crick Report has been widely cited as a key source for a critical understanding of the strengths and weaknesses of England's citizenship education at the time. The report usefully considered citizenship education in the then socio-political context of England and was a catalyst for much of what has happened since. The Group's terms of reference outlined the remit of citizenship education as:

> . . . the teaching of civics, participative democracy and citizenship, and may be taken to include some understanding of democratic practices and institutions, including parties, pressure groups and voluntary bodies, and the relationship of formal political activity with civic society in the context of the UK, Europe and the wider world . . . and . . . an element of the way in which expenditure and taxation work, together with a grasp of the underlying economic realities of adult life . . . [.] (p. 4)

Citizenship education was viewed as a response to a national agenda that had been established by the previous government in the introduction of the 1988 Education Reform Act. The Act outlined the need for a balanced curriculum that would prepare pupils 'for the opportunities, responsibilities and experiences of adult life'. The Crick Report recognised the multilingual and multicultural nature of England's society and the ensuing need to promote cultural awareness and understanding:

> . . . a main aim for the whole community should be to find or restore a sense of common citizenship, including a national identity that is secure enough to find a place for the plurality of nations, cultures, ethnic identities and religions long found in the United Kingdom. Citizenship education creates common ground between different ethnic and religious identities. (p. 17)
>
> The fourth national survey, Ethnic Minorities in Britain: Diversity and Disadvantage (Policy Studies Institute, 1997), recommended that 'an explicit idea of multi-cultural citizenship needs to be formulated for Britain' and that 'a more plural approach to racial disadvantage requires forms of citizenship which are sensitive to ethnic diversity and offer respect both to individuals and to the social groups to which they feel they belong'. (p. 17)

And in drawing implications for Ofsted, the Office for Standards in Education:

> (Section 5.3) – Pupils' Spiritual, Moral, Social and Cultural Development, requires inspectors to evaluate the extent to which the school encourages pupils to

relate positively to others, take responsibility, participate fully in the community, and develop an understanding of citizenship. (p. 30)

Nevertheless, the Crick Report made little reference to the role of language learning in developing citizenship. In the eighty-eight-page document, the Group refers to language learning only once: 'Modern Foreign Languages (MFL) can offer a contrasting perspective from other countries on National, European and international events and issues' (p. 53).

Professional development needs for teaching citizenship were recommended for history, geography and English teachers, but no mention was made of language teachers, seemingly under-exploring the potential language education offers for developing multilingual and multicultural conceptualisations of citizenship.

In the year 2000, the Nuffield Report was published, following an inquiry commissioned by the Nuffield Foundation, with a mandate to examine 'the UK's capability in languages and to report on what we need to do as a nation to improve it . . .' (p. 4). The report was framed principally in the context of the global job market and the economic climate. It argued that the United Kingdom's competitiveness was significantly threatened by the lack of language skills and suggested changing language attitudes among young professionals, a shortage of language skills among the UK workforce and the need for greater employment mobility, along with trade liberalisation, a shift towards service industries and technological advances enabling the rapid growth of small businesses as key social developments necessitating a language policy change. Moreover, the report cited changes in social values emphasising local and regional loyalties and a desire from incoming communities to both integrate into the surrounding society and preserve their own traditional cultures and languages. Finally, the report suggested that the increasingly mobile nature of families resulted in different expectations of the range of foreign languages that young generations would consider important. In short, the report viewed language learning as part and parcel of equipping young people to relate effectively and to prosper personally, socially and economically, in a dynamic and rapidly changing society.

The Nuffield Inquiry warned against the dangers of complacency that could arise from the globalisation of English, the damaging effects of monolingualism and the possible sense of 'inflexibility, insensitivity and arrogance' (p. 14) that monolingualism implies in a bilingual and multilingual world. In this context, the Nuffield Report made at least a brief reference to the relationship between multilingualism and the practice of citizenship: 'Much that is essential to our society, its health and its interests – including effective choice in policy, realisation of citizenship, effective overseas links and openness to the inventions of other cultures – will not be achieved in one language alone' (p. 14).

The report also promoted language learning as a means of fostering tolerance and respect:

> It is widely accepted that learning a new language can give the learner insights into how other people think, and engender respect for other cultures and ways

> of life. It can lead to more tolerant attitudes on a broader front, and to respect for other institutions and values, both within the UK and in the wider world. (Nuffield Report 2000, p. 30)

Language learning was thus explicitly linked to citizenship education in this report, promoting the kinds of cultural attitudes and values associated with cosmopolitan citizenship, specifically providing a means through which to combat an insular outlook. Yet, while citizenship associated with other curriculum areas, such as geography and history, has more explicitly addressed the need to prepare learners for the exercise of cosmopolitan citizenship, the role of language education has been more explicitly outlined in relation to, in this case, European citizenship, going hand in hand with a predominant focus on the learning of European languages rooted more in historical and political developments than in the lived realities of the learners. Even given this apparent preference for European citizenship, Morrell (1996) highlighted the limited inclusion of a European dimension in the National Curriculum for England and Wales at that time. The then Department for Education and Skills justified this by arguing that young people have a right to an education rooted in their own language and culture – a position that Morrell challenged, proposing instead that such education goes hand in hand with developing an understanding of the European and world context and the role of the United Kingdom and of British citizens within these contexts. Indeed, given the number of non-British European citizens who have settled in Britain and brought the European dimension into the heart of society, an education that ignores or neglects the European dimension, would, by definition, not be rooted in the reality of learners' own language and culture.

More recent decades saw a gradual development in England from reluctance to acceptance of a European dimension in the curriculum (Convey and Merritt 2000). Nevertheless, while several policy documents have pointed to this fact, as is often the case there has been a marked difference between policy and classroom reality, making the Brexit result less surprising. Of course, the Brexit outcome is a result of a complex interplay of factors. Nevertheless, education plays a vital role in educating and shaping the opinions and attitudes of young people. This was clearly recognised in the joint interim report of the Council and the European Commission, which set out the education and training objectives for 2010, re-stating the previously highlighted importance of the European dimension in formal education:

> School has a fundamental role to play allowing everyone to be informed and understand the meaning of European integration. All education systems should ensure that their pupils have, by the end of their secondary education, the knowledge and competences they need to prepare them for their role as future citizens in Europe. (Council of the European Union 2004: 42)

Within discussions of the integration of the European dimension, the role of language teaching has received some attention within the European Commission. The Green Paper on the European Dimension of Education (Commission of the

European Communities 1993, Art. 5, p. 3) cited linguistic competence as a key factor for facilitating young people's integration into society. Further, the 1995 White Paper on Education also promoted languages as key to the development of 'the feeling of being European', further stating 'multilingualism is part and parcel of both European identity/citizenship and the learning society' (European Commission 1995: 47).

Support for the role of language learning in promoting European citizenship was also evident in UK government policy reports. The House of Lords European Union Select Committee report (2005), for instance, suggested that language learning provides the means through which British young people might access the opportunities available through European Union membership. Echoing the Nuffield Inquiry, the report underlined the importance of linguistic competence in maintaining Britain's competitive edge in the labour market. The report went further, indicating that increased competition in the labour market underlined the need for effective interaction with those who are culturally different, at levels that would lead to cooperation and a deepened understanding of each other:

> We conclude that the United Kingdom is already falling badly behind in language-learning capability. This will seriously limit British ability to take part fully in and benefit from the new EU programmes . . . declining capacity for language-learning in this country [will have] far wider implications for the employability and cultural awareness of the coming generation and will severely hamper the country's ability to protect and promote our interests abroad and to compete successfully. (House of Lords European Union Select Committee 2005: 64)

Nevertheless, transferring this understanding into real classroom practice has been an ongoing challenge. Based on their research on pupils' perceptions of Europe, Convery et al. concluded:

> Young people consider themselves ill-served by a conservative and cautious curriculum and by a media unable to mediate the complexity of the issues. Apart from a few pockets of activity, evidence of learning about Europe at any level of sophistication is scarce'. (1997: 54)

Indeed, where young English people do associate language learning with citizenship practices, it is primarily in instrumental terms, as a tool enabling them to go to Europe on holiday or improve later job opportunities, rather than for the social benefits of better understanding the speakers of the language or its associated culture (Convery et al. 1997; Hennebry 2011). Perhaps this lack of sense of connectedness has played a part in the decision to part ways with Europe. In trying to understand what has led to a lack of intrinsic motivation among British young people, Convery et al. (1997) argued that the curriculum did little to 'transcend cultural barriers and fails to provide an environment for multiple identities' (p. 67).

Thus, we turn now to consider the Programmes of Study (PoS) for Modern Foreign Languages, in their current and former state.

## THE PROGRAMMES OF STUDY FOR LANGUAGE TEACHING

The PoS within England's existing National Curriculum for Languages is a considerably shorter document than its predecessor. Within the PoS for languages, both at Key Stage (KS) 2 (primary) and KS3 (secondary), the Department for Education (2013) outlines language learning as a means of attaining 'liberation from insularity' and providing 'an opening to other cultures'. Thus, through language learning the learner can connect and relate to the wider world and participate in the development of social cohesion as a result of greater interconnectedness. The document further outlines the purpose of language learning as fostering learners' curiosity and 'deepening their understanding of the world', suggesting that learners come to better understand the world they inhabit and with which they interact. Thus language learning is central to citizenship practice, and citizenship entails an understanding of and interaction with other cultures.

Unlike the previous PoS, the current PoS provides only general guidance as to what should be taught. In outlining some of the general skills that students should be taught, the KS3 PoS offers some opportunity for teachers to integrate aspects of citizenship, for instance enabling students to respond appropriately to language they have heard, to make use of important social conventions, or to expand their understanding of the language and culture. While these references seemingly allow flexibility for promoting citizenship themes, they do not necessarily translate this way in the classroom. Previous research suggests a considerable difference between language policy and classroom practice (Hennebry 2011). Significantly, despite the same preamble, the KS2 PoS offers less scope for integrating citizenship. This may be because of an assumption that certain levels of language proficiency are necessary in order for learners to engage with the more complex ideas associated with citizenship education. Nevertheless, KS2 represents for many learners their first point of contact with formal language learning, such that learning at this stage may have a deep impact on the remainder of their language learning trajectory. This first exposure can either promote the centrality of language learning to the lives they live and envision, or a view of language learning as another school subject consisting of decontextualised vocabulary lists and grammar rules to be learned, rehearsed and regurgitated.

Comparing the current PoS with their predecessors, the first striking difference is the detailed proscription of the former document in contrast with the brevity of today's PoS. One reason for this change was in order to offer schools and teachers greater freedom to exercise their professional understanding and expertise. Perhaps an advantage of the previous document, however, was the more explicit reference to matters of citizenship and the social development of the learner, raising teachers' awareness and making it more likely that such matters might be included in schemes of work, or at least would not be seen as irrelevant to language teaching.

The curriculum aims of the 2007 PoS reflected those of the wider National Curriculum. Among them, that all young people should become 'confident individuals who are able to live safe, healthy and fulfilling lives' and 'responsible citizens who make a positive contribution to society' (Qualifications and Curriculum Authority (QCA) 2007). These aims are clearly associated with citizenship development. Languages were seen as 'part of the cultural richness of our society and the world in which we live and work' (QCA 2007). Indeed, the document explicitly related language learning to citizenship: 'learning languages contributes to mutual understanding, a sense of global citizenship and personal fulfilment' (QCA 2007). Thus, language learning is more than acquiring a linguistic system and is instead a means through which learners participate in society, building relationship with others and working towards personal and social enrichment: 'Pupils learn to appreciate different countries, cultures, communities and people. By making comparisons they gain insight into their own culture and society' (QCA 2007: 3). The 2007 PoS explicitly conveyed a view of language learning as key to citizenship practice, equipping learners with the tools and attitudes for effective engagement with society. This civic conceptualisation was also built into the PoS key concepts, particularly *intercultural understanding*, stipulating that pupils should learn to appreciate 'the richness and diversity of other cultures', acknowledging 'different ways of seeing the world' and developing 'an international outlook' (QCA 2007).

This examination of the preamble of the former PoS points to an emphasis on integrating intercultural awareness and developing attitudes for cosmopolitan citizenship. However, this emphasis was limited to the preamble and the introductory framework. In stipulating the attainment targets and levels learners should work towards, the focus was exclusively on the four skills (reading, writing, listening and speaking), grammatical awareness and accuracy and accurate communication of meaning. Even at the highest attainment levels, there was no mention of cultural awareness, the need to use language in a culturally respectful manner, with understanding of the target language communities and their values or the ability to compare cultural norms. Research evidence suggests that this omission has played a key part in the exclusion of planned citizenship development from the language classroom (Hennebry 2014). Of course, topics stipulated in the former PoS – such as the family, the environment, my town, etc. – might all be taught in ways that integrate related aspects of citizenship; for instance: the cultural diversity in my town and the richness as well as complexity that brings, the changes in the ways we have traditionally conceptualised the family, the need to be an environmentally responsible citizen, etc., all of these offer potential for critical reflection on the roles of the individual in society and the ways in which linguistic competence might allow enactment of these roles. However, teachers who feel constrained by an overcrowded curriculum and a heavy exam performance orientation find little time to engage with citizenship aspects that are neither integrated in the curriculum nor required in language assessment. Hennebry (2014) pointed to teachers' desire to engage with language teaching that goes beyond the development of linguistic structures to consider language in a broader sense, as a means of real communication across cultural communities:

> You're trying to say it can get you out of your little box and make you see that there's something bigger out there . . . (P. 296)

> I think a lot of the kids they just don't realise that the people who speak these languages actually exist; they think it's just us teaching something. I would like to do a lot more culture but we just tend to go through the curriculum. (P. 299)

> If they could see it as one big Europe and we all need to be speaking different languages it's certainly going to make my job as a language teacher so much easier because they would see the point . . . if we did more culture with them I think that would have a big impact on their desire to learn. (P. 299)

> Knowing a language, knowing oneself, always leads one to recognise the importance of knowing other people, other cultures, another reality. (P. 299)

> Without a doubt . . . that would help to overcome nationalism and narrow-mindedness and it could even provide a means of resolving conflict. (P. 298)

> You know, in my ideal world they would come to school they would learn a bit of geography within their language, as in they would come and learn France as well as French within my subject, we wouldn't just do the language, we'd find out about the art, we'd find out about the food, we'd find out about the geography . . . we'd learn about what it actually means to be French, why we'd want to be in France and therefore it would become . . . (P. 297)

Nevertheless, teachers perceived a number of obstacles, from learners' limited language proficiency:

> It's almost a vicious circle, that before you can look at cultural stuff and particular authentic materials on a particular topic . . . they need to reach a certain level of German and so you're actually trying to build their language up but they're doing that out of context so contextualizing is a tricky part of it but it's very important. (P. 301)

to the perceived constraints of the National Curriculum:

> . . . it's become horribly tight and to do with jumping through hoops frankly. It is all about what's a subordinate clause, have I included one, have you got three tenses there, have you made your verbs agree, have you made your adjectives agree . . . certainly it's not about learning the culture or citizenship of countries in Europe. (P. 302)

and a lack of time:

> Creativity is what's missing and with that could come more of a cultural understanding but if you stop what you're doing so that you can do a little project on whatever it is, then when you next come to try and do it there's even less time for it and the trend is towards compressing the languages curriculum. (P. 302)

Teachers in the study highlighted the considerable disparity they found in the classroom reality between policy and practice. While the obstacles teachers identified may be also a matter of perception, the development of citizenship through language teaching cannot and will not be a reality unless teachers receive adequate support, training, resources, adequate amounts of time to reflect on language pedagogy for citizenship, and a curriculum and assessment aligned with these citizenship aims. In the case of England which we are now analysing, and in light of the recent move away from the European Union, the United Kingdom will need to give careful thought to the ways in which education promotes a form of citizenship that forges international relationships. To this end, it will probably become increasingly important to consider ways in which the languages curriculum might offer spaces for promoting some of the essential notions accompanying the intercultural and cosmopolitan citizen, in ways that are both feasible and integrated into the broader assessment framework, in order to start repositioning the country in its new chosen place within the community of nations.

## HONG KONG

Hong Kong's linguistic context is both similar to and distinct from that of England. Both contexts are multilingual and characterised by rich cultural diversity. In some important ways, however, the contexts differ. Firstly, while the United Kingdom voted to leave their supra-national, regional enclave, in this case the European Union, moving towards a separatist position, Hong Kong is adapting to a closer union with Mainland China. This context is important because while separation from the European Union might seemingly challenge the previous emphasis on learning European languages, the handover process for Hong Kong has meant explicit and widespread language policy change that has seen the systematic introduction of Mandarin teaching across schools since 1998. Indeed, in 1999, the Education Bureau began to publicise its long-term goal of adopting Putonghua, rather than Cantonese, as the medium of instruction in Chinese classes. About a decade later, the HKSAR Standing Committee on Language Education and Research announced its intention to provide US$26 million to schools that switched from Mandarin as the medium of instruction for Chinese classes. The Education Bureau stated on its website that Cantonese was not an official language, but rather a Chinese dialect; a statement they later recanted.

Language policy in Hong Kong is a rich area of study, though the time and space constraints of this chapter do not allow for a full exploration of the topic here.

A key point to note, however, is that Hong Kong provides an example of a context where the choice of language for instruction and the languages that are taught have been and are heavily influenced by the kind of citizenship its government wishes to promote and the kind of socio-political forces that have been at play in its society during this recent period of its history. Thus, English continues to be an official language in Hong Kong and is by far the most commonly taught second language in schools, having been identified as a key curriculum learning area. Meanwhile, the government encourages biliteracy in Chinese and English and trilingualism in English, Cantonese and Mandarin, and continues to promote the use of Mandarin also as a medium of instruction. Current government figures report that, in 2016, 89.5 per cent of the population were native Cantonese speakers, 3.5 per cent were speakers of English, 1.38 per cent were Putonghua (Mandarin) speakers, 4.02 per cent were speakers of other Chinese dialects and 1.57 per cent of the population spoke other languages (Hong Kong Government 2016). However, this linguistic landscape may change considerably in the coming years given the transition from British to Chinese rule. Hong Kong's emphasis on the learning of English specifically as a tool for effective social participation and global competitiveness, raises interesting questions about the shaping of Hong Kong's identity at a time of transition that would benefit from future research.

Hong Kong's curriculum guide for English Language Education (ELE) is considerably more detailed than England's two-page document. The document situates ELE in the wider curriculum framework, outlines the role of ELE in promoting positive social values, provides guidance on curriculum planning, pedagogical strategies and assessment, points teachers to useful teaching and learning resources, and offers examples for putting into practice the guidance offered in the document. This occurs in sharp contrast with England, where second language learning is no longer a compulsory part of the school curriculum. ELE in Hong Kong is a Key Learning Area (KLA), an integral part of the school curriculum since it is seen to contribute to students' 'cultural understanding' and their 'global competitiveness' (Curriculum Development Council (CDC) 2002). A KLA in the context of the Hong Kong curriculum is considered a *major field of knowledge which should be acquired by all students*. These KLAs are contexts within which learners can both develop and apply generic skills such as collaboration and critical thinking. As a KLA, ELE is expected to:

> . . . develop learners' English proficiency for study, work and leisure; provide them with opportunities for personal and intellectual development; extend their knowledge and experience of other cultures through the English medium and help them overcome the challenges of the rapidly changing and keenly competitive knowledge-based society of Hong Kong.

Thus, ELE is seen as central to the whole-person development of the learner, as further emphasised by the CDC Chairman (Education Bureau 2001):

> The school curriculum, apart from helping students to acquire necessary knowledge, should also help the younger generation . . . to learn and to master lifelong skills that can be used outside schools. The curriculum should also cultivate students' positive values and attitudes and achieve the educational aims of promoting whole-person development and lifelong learning. (Education Bureau 2001: 4)

In the context of the curriculum, positive values refer, for instance, to *quality*, *interdependence* and *tolerance* as well as *responsibility*, *open-mindedness* and *cooperativeness* (Education Bureau 2001: 22), values that are seen as crucial to the healthy development of the learner.

The stated aims of ELE are to:

- . . . provide every learner of a second language with further opportunities for extending their knowledge and experience of the cultures of other people as well as opportunities for personal and intellectual development, further studies, pleasure and work in the English medium;
- . . . enable every learner to prepare for the changing socio-economic demands resulting from advances in information technology . . . (Curriculum Development Council and the Hong Kong Examinations and Assessment Authority 2007: 2)

Schools are encouraged to enrich the teaching and learning of English language by incorporating 'moral and civic education' and using literary texts as a tool for promoting 'critical thinking and encourag[ing] free expression and creativity' – skills that are central to active citizenship. The guide specifically encourages schools and teachers to work towards developing 'an open-minded attitude towards difference cultures, ideologies and points of view . . .' (Curriculum Development Council 2017: 222) as well as to 'enrich and extend students' language learning experiences in real contexts and authentic settings through English-related life-wide learning activities' (p. 32). Thus, language learning is viewed not only as the means through which learners develop attitudes for effective intercultural interaction, but also as integral to everyday life and society.

Perhaps the most significant and explicit way in which the curriculum illustrates a relationship between ELE and citizenship development is by reference to the ways in which the values and attitudes incorporated as part of the broader curriculum might be promoted through ELE. This constitutes an extensive section of the curriculum guide and it is not possible to review it in detail in this chapter, though it is helpful to consider some indicative examples.

The values that are integrated into the curriculum (Curriculum Development Council 2017: 219) are:

<table>
<tr><th>Core values: Personal</th><th>Core values: Social</th><th>Attitudes</th></tr>
<tr><td>Sanctity of life<br>Truth<br>Aesthetics<br>Honesty<br>Human dignity<br>Rationality<br>Creativity<br>Courage<br>Liberty<br>Affectivity<br>Individuality</td><td>Equality<br>Kindness<br>Benevolence<br>Love<br>Freedom<br>Common good<br>Mutuality<br>Justice<br>Trust<br>Interdependence<br>Sustainability<br>Betterment of human kind</td><td rowspan="3">Optimistic<br>Participatory<br>Critical<br>Creative<br>Appreciative<br>Empathetic<br>Caring<br>Positive<br>Confident<br>Cooperative<br>Responsible<br>Adaptable to changes<br>Open-minded<br>With respect for:<br>– self<br>– others<br>– life<br>– quality and excellence<br>– evidence<br>– fair play<br>– rule of law<br>– different ways of life, beliefs and opinions<br>– the environment<br>With a desire to learn<br>Diligent<br>Committed to core and sustaining values</td></tr>
<tr><td>Sustaining values: Personal</td><td>Sustaining values: Social</td></tr>
<tr><td>Self-esteem<br>Self-reflection<br>Self-discipline<br>Self-cultivation<br>Principled morality<br>Self-determination<br>Openness</td><td>Plurality<br>Due process of law<br>Democracy<br>Freedom and liberty<br>Common will<br>Patriotism<br>Tolerance<br>Equal opportunities<br>Culture and civilisation heritage<br>Human rights and responsibilities<br>Rationality<br>Sense of belonging<br>Solidarity</td></tr>
</table>

The curriculum guide proposes that ELE can promote all of these values through specific learning objectives at each Key Stage. For instance, at KS1, these values are promoted through the following examples of implementation (Curriculum Development Council 2017: 220):

- develop confidence in using English through performing tasks individually or in groups, etc.
- show keenness to participate in activities leading to improvement of knowledge and skills in the language and not worry about making mistakes
- develop sensitivity towards language use in the process of communication
- appreciate the beauty of the language through enjoying singing English songs and reading simple rhymes, etc.
- show care and concern towards others through expressing good wishes
- participate actively and work with others to complete a task, respecting their rights

- develop self-motivation through telling the teacher their feelings concerning English learning in general and in specific tasks
- evaluate their own learning through reviewing samples of their writing over time and note the improvement or lack of it in areas such as accuracy and the organisation of ideas
- distinguish between positive and negative values.

A similar outline is provided at KS2, 3 and 4. While some of the examples might apply similarly across other curriculum areas, the objectives also acknowledge that language learning offers unique opportunities not so readily available in other subject areas. For instance at KS1, students should learn to: *appreciate the beauty of the language*; at KS2: *show understanding and respect for the different cultures of the English-speaking world through participating in learning activities concerning themes of other places* (p. 221); at KS3: *develop an awareness of the potential influences . . . of language use on other people's feelings and direction of thinking* (p. 223); and at KS4: *develop through language learning activities . . . an open-minded attitude towards different cultures, ideologies and points of view and a willingness to share ideas with different people* (p. 223).

While topics to be covered are not specified in this document, suggestions are made in other documents such as the English Language Curriculum and Assessment Guide for Secondary 4–6, and include: *Getting along with others (friendship and dating; sharing, cooperation, rivalry)*; *Cultures of the world (travelling and visiting; customs, clothes and food of different places)*; *The individual and society (crime; human rights (personal rights, civic rights, respect))*. Topics such as this offer rich opportunities for promoting citizenship both at the local and global level.

The curriculum guide explicitly and in considerable detail links language learning to the promotion of active citizenship, making it clear that language learning is more than simply grammar and vocabulary systems; rather it is a primary means of socialisation. In contrast to England's language curriculum, Hong Kong's curriculum for English offers considerably more detailed guidance for the ways in which ELE can and should promote the values and attitudes that underpin active citizenship, perhaps suggesting echoes of the Chinese influence. ELE is thus viewed as a key component of the curriculum and of the whole-person development for a cohesive and competitive society.

Given the extensive and detailed integration of citizenship themes into the curriculum guide for ELE in Hong Kong, a useful research direction would be to examine the extent to which this has filtered down to the classrooms in Hong Kong, where the assessment orientation is as strong if not stronger than that in England and where language assessment focuses almost exclusively on linguistic form rather than on content. In some ways language curricula are to be considered a compass rather than a recipe book, in that they point towards a direction and provide a framework within which to walk. However, a key factor needed to start fulfilling the curriculum aims resides in delivering the curriculum in a way that is faithful to these aims by equipping teachers with the necessary knowledge and skills and bringing them on board with the endeavour. Top-down implementation of curriculum delivery rarely succeeds without considerable buy-in from the teacher practitioners.

This chapter has examined the positioning of language education in relation to citizenship in England and Hong Kong, highlighting the role of socio-historical and socio-political contexts in shaping language policy at this level. In doing so it points to the way in which language education priorities and orientations shaped and are shaped by their social context, such that language curricula can be a means through which to respond to political relations and emerging socio-economic needs.

**For reflection**

This chapter has highlighted the interplay that can exist between socio-historical events and the shape of language education. The prevalence of English in the Hong Kong curriculum is, for example, to a large extent the result of Hong Kong's history with Great Britain.

- ➢ Can you identify any key socio-historical developments that you think have influenced the shape of language attitudes and the language curriculum in your own context?
- ➢ How do you think language teachers should respond pedagogically to socio-historical developments?
- ➢ What role do you think language education should play, if any, in these developments?

## NOTE

1. A White Paper is the means through which the British government announces policy preferences in advance of introducing legislation. It provides a tool through which to gauge public opinion on given issues.

# Chapter 7

# Cosmopolitan citizenship and English language teaching

**Objectives**

- To engage with extended discussion of cosmopolitan and global citizenship and compare and contrast these two.
- To understand the relationship between debates surrounding English language learning and teaching, and concepts of cosmopolitan and global citizenship.
- To understand the relevance of a critical pedagogies' paradigm to issues of cosmopolitan and global citizenship.

## INTRODUCTION

In earlier chapters we explored the concept of citizenship at both national and European levels. This chapter is devoted to considering how citizenship might be defined and enacted at a more global level, looking at the literature on both cosmopolitan and global citizenship (and indeed the overlap between them), taking further some of the points raised in Chapter 3 that covered citizenship at a global level in the higher education domain, as well as other references we have already made to cosmopolitan citizenship. We cover existing theoretical and empirical research which has aligned itself with one of these terms specifically, although we acknowledge the substantial interconnectivity in the way the two often tend to be deployed. We cover issues such as how cosmopolitan and global citizenship interact with English language teaching; how the globalisation of the learning, teaching and use of the English language impacts on our understandings of citizenship; how conceptualisations such as English as a lingua franca (ELF) and Global Englishes (GEs) may play a role in expressing cosmopolitan citizenship, and indeed challenging the linguistic identity of native English speakers; and, finally, an exploration of critical pedagogies in the context of English language teaching, and how such a pedagogical approach may facilitate the exploration of linguistic and cultural identities, and indeed cosmopolitan citizenship. A predominant aim of this chapter is to develop an understanding of the sorts of arguments that have been made about the limitations of supra-national concepts of citizenship, to be able to further develop critical thinking skills on this issue. However, our presentation of these debates should not be seen as undermining much of what we have outlined elsewhere in the book, namely explorations of how citizenship at a range of levels can meaningfully underpin language teaching. In this chapter, we merely seek to present a multifaceted argument.

## EXPLORING COSMOPOLITAN AND GLOBAL CITIZENSHIP

We have previously made reference to the notion of cosmopolitan citizenship at various junctures; in this section, we devote attention to the conceptualisation of this notion in the literature. Osler and Starkey (2003: 246–247) outlined in detail some key tenets that they believe are fundamental to the idea of cosmopolitan citizenship. They specify that a main role adopted by an 'educated cosmopolitan citizen' is one of building harmony at both a local level and beyond, taking actions that are largely underpinned by a social justice ethos. In being aware of one's own perspectives, the educated cosmopolitan citizen is then able to value diversity in others. In their coverage of literature on conceptualising cosmopolitan citizenship, Boni and Calabuig (2017) agree that there should necessarily be a focus on encouraging critical self-awareness, as a foundation from which individuals can then engage in a respectful way with the inevitable differences among people in a given society, and, indeed, can show sufficient empathy to another by being able to put themselves in someone else's position to gain respect for alternative perspectives.

In terms of why we should be considering citizenship beyond national borders, Osler and Starkey argue that in a world which is ever more interconnected, conceptualising citizens and citizenship at merely the national level would be an oversimplification: 'all human lives are increasingly influenced by events in other parts of the world . . . If democracy is now conceptualised as cosmopolitan, then the actors within the democracy are, by extension, cosmopolitan citizens' (2003: 246). As Osler and Starkey claim, any reconceptualisation of citizenship as it exists and is enacted at the national level has been driven largely by processes of globalisation – there is much agreement about this in the literature. Staeheli, for example, agrees with this assertion but places emphasis on the abstract nature of 'cosmopolitan' or 'global' citizenship, arguing instead that there is still a powerful role played by a somewhat more tangible sense of citizenship at the national level: 'For all the discussion of worlds without borders and the hollowing of the nation-state that has accompanied the strong globalization hypothesis, the nation-state remains the location in which the formal aspects of citizenship are structured' (Staeheli 1999: 72).

A pertinent example of this is the increasing prevalence of discourses relating to 'internationalisation' within higher education, a point we raised in Chapter 3. Coryell, Spencer and Sehin (2014: 146) explain that it is within such discourses that the notion of the 'global citizen' often becomes emphasised and enacted, as a means of meeting higher education institutions' goals of facilitating their students to become global citizens. As they explain, the notion of 'global citizenship' interacts with that of 'cosmopolitanism' or 'cosmopolitan citizenship', in that the latter relates to engaging with a 'shared global community' (Langran 2011: 4). Similarly, Boni and Calabuig (2017: 25) claim that in certain bodies of literature 'global citizenship' and 'cosmopolitan citizenship' can be deployed interchangeably. Indeed, there is a growing body of empirical work exploring how such concepts may be defined and enacted, by a range of key stakeholders, in the context of (the internationalisation of) higher education. Recent examples include Coryell, Spencer and Sehin (2014), Aktas et al. (2017), Boni and Calabuig (2017), Kahn and Agnew (2017) and Lilley, Barker and Harris (2017). In their exploration of how the global citizen may be conceptualised by key stakeholders in the internationalisation of higher education in different regions of the world, Lilley et al. address previous literature (see for example Appadurai 2000; Appiah 2006; and Schattle 2008) which has considered the extent to which constructs such as 'cosmopolitanism' and the 'global citizen' are comprised of core values which are dealt with in major world religions, 'namely, openness, tolerance, respect, and responsibility toward others' (Lilley, Barker and Harris 2017: 8). Lilley, Barker and Harris draw the conclusion that such core values are thus to some degree universal (being inherent to a diverse range of world religions), and therefore have the potential to transcend cultural boundaries, and can facilitate globally mobile students adding new facets to their identities.

There is scope, however, for interpreting Lilley, Barker and Harris' conclusion differently. Jooste and Heleta (2017) criticise global citizenship as a concept for its lack of innovation; rather, they argue, it simply acts as an umbrella term for a range of positive characteristics (for example 'basic common sense and human decency, social responsibility, and good critical thinking skills, coupled with the knowledge, awareness, and care for global issues' (p. 45)). Even more problematic than its failure to provide to the higher education setting anything that has not already been seen before is its promulgation of inequity and injustice, reinforcing what they understand as structures of 'north-south' power imbalances. The concept of global citizenship enables:

> . . . a creation of a new 'learned' elite known as global citizens who are open-minded and enlightened, unlike their 'close-minded,' 'nationalistic,' and 'tribalistic' peers who apparently do not care about the people or world beyond their ethnic or religious groups or outside the borders of their countries. (Ibid.)

Further, Jooste and Heleta make clear their stance that globalisation – and the related concept of global citizenship – is seen as relevant and positive by those in countries embodying positions of power; they argue that being guided by such ideologies has the potential to be harmful to less powerful countries, however. With specific reference to global citizenship in the context of the internationalisation of higher education, they state that:

> The global citizenship movement, like cosmopolitanism, hails from the Western world, tends to be elitist, and is practiced and promoted by those with the ability and means to travel and engage around the globe (Andreotti, 2006).

> [Cosmopolitans and global citizens] are "generally antinationalist, seeing nations as part of the fading order of political life divided on lines of states" (Calhoun, 2003, p. 535). Yet, these "citizens of the world" who claim to be beyond nations continue to hold closely onto their country's citizenship and passports, which protect them and facilitate easy travel around the world (particularly if they are from the global North). Despite their claims and/or desires, global citizens "are neither beyond not above the states." Their ambitions "remain dependent upon the capacity of states to provide and guarantee a secure base" (Bowden, 2003, p. 360). Thus, the large majority of the "global citizens" still have strong allegiance to their countries and communities, pay local and national taxes, with their allegiance to humanity as a whole being not more than half-empty rhetoric. (Jooste and Heleta 2017: 42–43)

The important point to take from this excerpt is the paradox that those in powerful positions by dint of their national citizenship are free to explore the more abstract concept of global citizenship, while continuing to enjoy the myriad benefits offered by their national citizenship: global citizenship is a luxury for those already privileged to access. On the other hand, for individuals from less powerful nation states, Jooste and Heleta claim that exploring somewhat nebulous discourses is one that is either impossible, or at the very least unhelpful; more beneficial is concrete training in how to navigate an unequal global society (2017: 46).

Other authors have also considered possible drawbacks of cosmopolitan and global citizenship, some of which relate closely to the issues that Jooste and Heleta raise. In her discussion of global citizenship in higher education from a critical applied linguistics perspective, Henderson (2013: 8) claims that thorough conceptualisations of global citizenship necessarily need to take into account how students might begin to address issues of (cultural and linguistic) dominance, imbalances of power, and inherent structures of elitism that facilitate a minority, rather than a majority, to benefit. In their evaluation of programmes in higher education institutions which seek to explicitly address global citizenship, Aktas et al. (2017) discuss the common element among many of these curricula of seeking learning experiences outside the classroom, often in conjunction with international travel. While many higher education institutions promote this as a positive experience for students to undergo, Aktas et al. (2017: 74) question whether such opportunities for students in more developed nations (perhaps those that Jooste and Heleta would term 'more powerful' countries) actually serve to reinforce problematic structures of dominance:

> Certain types of engagement, for instance, may carry the potential to replicate social inequalities and promote, rather than dispel, damaging stereotypes. This becomes especially concerning considering the growing popularity of university level global citizenship programs in "developed" Western countries. These programs stereotypically see highly educated, economically stable, predominantly Caucasian individuals attempting to "save the world" by offering their services to

> "helpless" children in less developed Third World countries. (Aktas et al. 2017: 74)

Some further consideration of these limitations will be explored in more depth later on in this chapter.

Similar to Henderson, many have stressed that defining this abstract concept is a complex and problematic task (e.g. Coryell, Spencer and Sehin 2014; Boni and Calabuig 2017: 23; Jooste and Heleta 2017). Jooste and Heleta discuss how it has commonly been conceptualised as a sense of civic duty that transcends national borders. They raise the critique applied to this construct that for there to be a meaningful global citizenship, there should necessarily be some kind of global governing body (a point raised also by Osler 2016: 42), which they are strongly against (Jooste and Heleta 2017: 41). Furthermore, they explain that global citizenship being treated as an 'identity' or 'state of mind' (2017: 40) may well be at odds with higher education institutions that wish to incorporate this term into scholarly activities, but do not necessarily see their role as one being involved with identity construction (De Wit et al. 2013). Coryell, Spencer and Sehin's work also considers global citizenship in the context of higher education: they talk about how their participants in postgraduate study-abroad programmes conceptualise global citizenship as linking closely to the idea of being an effective cross-cultural communicator, being able to achieve professional goals in a range of cultural contexts (2014: 156). Lilley, Barker and Harris have also investigated global citizenship in the higher education setting, and argue that ambiguous definitions of the global citizen concept have made it difficult to incorporate into pedagogical approaches (Lilley, Barker and Harris 2017: 9). Their participants' views are similar to those in Coryell, Spencer and Sehin's study, in that much focus was placed on cross-cultural communication; Lilley, Barker and Harris' (2017: 12–13) participants spoke specifically of 'moral values congruent with openness, tolerance, respect, and responsibility for self, others, and the planet'.

An important implication drawn from this research was the idea that while terminology may differ in how such an abstract concept is defined, there is nonetheless broad consensus in how such ideals may be achieved:

> This research suggests that problematizing how all students can learn to become global citizens is more important than focusing on rigid definitions. . . . The majority of participants supported a plural global identity for the global citizen in higher education. By understanding their evolving hybrid identity (Luke & Luke, 2000; Rhoads & Szelenyi, 2011), students are better equipped to think and imagine the transmission of ideas, media, and cultures across porous global boundaries and in their communities. (Lilley, Barker and Harris 2017: 15)

Although it appears from research such as that from Lilley, Barker and Harris that global citizenship in education is being considered in an in-depth way, Aktas et al. (2017: 66) make the point that some educational institutions have a more superficial rather than a deep approach to global citizenship, and it is with this in mind that they seek to analyse mission statements of programmes that relate to global citizenship. As we have mentioned in earlier chapters, critical thinking and reflection has often been stated as being a necessary underpinning of enacting citizenship, and this is a stance that Aktas et al. align themselves with. Another crucial finding from these authors relates to language proficiency requirements within global citizenship programmes. As they note, 'None of the programs explicitly talked about the importance of knowing more than one language or discussed it as essential to being a global citizen' (Aktas et al. 2017: 72). Again, this link between explorations of citizenship and language learning is one we have covered elsewhere. What is worth noting here is the seeming lack of acknowledgement within Aktas et al.'s dataset of the relationship between global citizenship and competence in more than one language, which we would argue is a substantial oversight. Indeed, Aktas et al. agree with this, claiming that knowing more than one language is a vital part of the 'transformative' aspect of global citizenship, as well as it being a crucial skill in transcending borders and boundaries. In seeking to explain their finding, they propose that it may well be related to the global dominance of English as a language in the academic domain, but invoke arguments which build on Phillipson's (1992) thesis of 'linguistic imperialism' in explaining how potentially limiting, if not damaging, a failure to critically engage with the dominance of English could be for students seeking to become global citizens (Aktas et al. 2017: 73).

Having brought the discussion around to the role that language, and specifically English, may play in global citizenship, we now move on to considering specifically how a focus on English teaching and learning has factored into thinking about citizenship beyond national levels.

## COSMOPOLITAN CITIZENSHIP, GLOBAL CITIZENSHIP AND LANGUAGE LEARNING

We have talked in detail about the links between language and citizenship elsewhere. However, here we seek to extend this discussion to a consideration of the role of language in citizenship that transcends national borders, namely, cosmopolitan citizenship and global citizenship. In relation to research by Aktas et al. (2017) we have already laid the foundations for developing an argument about the important role that language may play; here, we consider this idea in more detail.

Similar to Aktas et al.'s findings about the role of language learning in global citizenship to be seen by many universities as minimal, if not non-existent, Kahn and Agnew (2017: 59) approach language in quite an incidental way. In their discussion of global learning and internationalising higher education curricula they acknowledge that an important part of such approaches is facilitating learners experiencing paradigm shifts by moving beyond the familiar to the unknown, and that one way of doing so is learning other languages. However, placing much more of a focus on the role of languages and language education, in developing what they term 'cosmopolitan citizenship', are Osler and Starkey (2015). Languages, they say, are a fundamental part of 'education for cosmopolitan citizenship', which is a way of doing citizenship in the classroom 'which addresses citizenship at a range of scales and which is explicitly linked to human rights principles and standards' (Osler and Starkey 2015: 31). What languages and citizenship education have in common, they say, are principles of critically reflecting on, appreciating, engaging with, and coping with, diversity (ibid.) – this is consistent with our discussion in Chapter 3 of such commonalities. Importantly, they believe that this process necessitates an understanding of the self as a precursor to understanding the other, because '[a]ll of us are making some kind of judgement or evaluation when we encounter a new cultural context, whether this positioning is acknowledged or not' (ibid.). It is worth noting that their conceptualisation of 'education for cosmopolitan citizenship' (and the role of language within this) is not the same as 'global citizenship education', as they are keen to stress. 'Education for global citizenship' is founded on principles of understanding the self, and indeed characteristics that may be shared across human beings (regardless of cultural/religious/linguistic backgrounds, for example), as well as understanding traditionally held conceptions of national identities (that is to say, holding a view of the nation itself being cosmopolitan (Osler 2005)):

> We define [education for cosmopolitan citizenship] as a status deriving from equal entitlement to human rights. It is based on a feeling of belonging and recognition of diversity across a range of communities from the local to the global. It is a practice of involving negotiation, equitable resolution of differences and work with others to promote freedom, justice and peace within and between communities (Osler and Starkey, 2005a). (Osler and Starkey 2015: 32)

What education for cosmopolitan citizenship and language education have in common, they say, is that to engage with cultural diversity in a surface or even disparaging way is problematic for the aims embedded within both (Osler and Starkey 2015: 35). In more detail, they explain:

> The skills developed in language classes are . . . directly transferable to citizenship education (Osler and Starkey, 2005[b]). In particular the language class is a site where education for dialogue is especially developed including skills such as the ability to listen, to reformulate the words of another the better to understand them, to put a different point of view, to produce a valid argument, to concede the strengths of someone else's position or perspective. (Ibid.)

This excerpt makes clear the potential for tightly integrating notions of citizenship beyond national borders, and language teaching and learning. Porto, Houghton and Byram (2017: 2) make a bold claim in this respect: 'language teaching can and should contribute to educational processes, to the development of individuals and to the evolution of societies'. They argue that when it is acknowledged that language education has high value in terms of its 'educational function', as well as more pragmatic benefits that may be accrued (what may be termed more 'instrumental' reasons for language learning, to go back to Gardner's motivational framework, outlined in Chapter 4), then the goals of language education neatly overlap with those of citizenship education (Porto, Houghton and Byram 2017: 2). Despite the rather natural crossover between the two domains, these authors nonetheless highlight possible challenges which need to be overcome for educators seeking to integrate them. They include: ensuring that critical reflection skills are sufficiently foregrounded; wider power issues relating to definition, and indeed dominance, of the native speaker (see Davies 2003), and ownership of language (discussed in more detail later on in this chapter), instead focusing on an 'intercultural speaker' rather than a native speaker; considerations of how best to move beyond the constraints of national identities in relation to global citizenship and language learning; and, finally, how being active within a community can be facilitated from both of these perspectives as well.

Discussed so far have been arguments supporting the integration of notions of cosmopolitan and/or global citizenship, and language education. Taking a slightly different tack is Henderson (2013), who seeks to explore the potential for integrating global citizenship and applied linguistics in higher education. In order to explore and exploit the overlap between the two domains, she raises the following questions:

- in what ways can the dominance of fixed inner circle English in the academy be reduced by an insistence on the development of more hybrid cultural and linguistic identities in course design and assessment?
- how can we use the cultural and linguistic wealth of our multilingual students in such ways that we allow all students to understand that inner circle English and its class values are not inherently superior to hybrid varieties of English and more cosmopolitan and radical values?
- in what ways can we alert our students to the traces of different discourses and ideologies in today's ever more multimodal texts and practices, including our own, so that they can explore the on-going imperative of speaking and writing back to power?
- how can we collaborate with students to transform and redesign our local and global social worlds for the benefit of all rather than the elite few?
- by what means can we demonstrate to our students that our theories of discourse, power and identity are not simply add-ons to their everyday practices, but vital tools for constructing a present and future social justice? (Henderson 2013: 8)

A number of themes emerge here which we have touched upon previously. For example, Henderson agrees with Aktas et al. (2017) and Porto, Houghton and Byram (2017) that issues surrounding the global dominance of English in the academic domain are a pressing issue; the 'hybrid cultural and linguistic identities' will be dealt with next in this chapter, in our consideration of ELF, and GEs. Her discussion of appreciation and valuing of multiplicity (in this case, multilingualism) has again been discussed at length in earlier chapters. Seeking to ensure positive outcomes for the many rather than the few, and indeed the relationship between citizenship and social justice, has been covered at various junctures, and specifically in this chapter with reference to Jooste and Heleta (2017).

Picking up on questions relating to the learning and teaching of English, we now turn our attention to English around the world, with specific focus on GEs and ELF, and implications for citizenship, in the following section.

## ENGLISH AROUND THE WORLD, AND IMPLICATIONS FOR CITIZENSHIP

We have already mentioned on a number of occasions issues relating to English as a foreign language (EFL). However, in this section we turn our attention to ELF. The difference between the two has been clearly laid out by Jenkins, Cogo and Dewey:

> ELF is part of the GLOBAL ENGLISHES paradigm, according to which most speakers of English are non-native speakers (henceforth NNSEs), and all English varieties, native or non-native, are accepted in their own right rather than evaluated against a NSE benchmark. By contrast, EFL is part of the MODERN (FOREIGN) LANGUAGES paradigm, according to which most interaction involving non-native speakers is with native speakers of the language, and non-native speakers' goal is to approximate the native variety as closely as possible. (2011: 283–284)

We are interested in this way of conceptualising the role of English globally given its potential for understanding and ascribing value to the diverse means of linguistic expression for those who identify as global citizens. A recent example of empirical work which has sought to understand the relationship between global citizenship identities and English language use is Sung (2016), who has explored expressions of global identities through ELF, in a Hong Kong university context where both students and faculty members represent a diverse range of linguistic and cultural backgrounds, and therefore where English is the primary means of lingua franca communication both inside and outside the classroom (Sung 2016: 307). In interviews with seven undergraduate students whose first language was Cantonese, but who were used to communicating also through English, it emerged that the capacity for ELF communication with a multilingual and multicultural student body facilitated a sense of a global identity and indeed global citizenship, by sharing perspectives on world events with those from different backgrounds (Sung 2016: 309). Furthermore, this interaction enabled students to develop a greater tolerance and appreciation for the different ways that the English language can be used, which perhaps may be characterised as 'non-standard'. Sung states that 'the participants seemed to display open-minded and tolerant attitudes toward linguistic diversity in ELF communication and considered such an attitude an important attribute of their global identities' (ibid.). He explicitly claims that a conclusion to be drawn from this qualitative study is the strength of the relationship between ELF communication and the development of a sense of being a global citizen, with the possibility of maintaining simultaneously a local (in this case, Hong Kong) identity, while laying claim to one that also goes beyond a local context:

> In claiming their global identities in ELF communication, the participants indicated their desires to express identification with the wider global community which went beyond their national and/or cultural identities associated with their L1. Instead of espousing narrow nationalist conceptualisations of identity, they took on identities as globally oriented citizens who claim membership in a supra-local community of people who share similar transcendent values, interests, concerns and experiences . . . Furthermore, the analysis indicates that the participants seemed to view multilingualism and/or plurilingualism as the norm in ELF communication. (Sung 2016: 311–312)

In Sung's summative discussion of his research findings, we see emerge again the viewpoint of multiplicity being viewed as a positive, rather than a negative or even dangerous, characteristic: this relates closely to discussions presented in Chapter 3. Furthermore, this appreciation of diversity is also a foundational tenet of Osler and Starkey's (2015: 31) views on how language teaching should interact with education for cosmopolitan citizenship. In earlier chapters, we have identified the crossover between citizenship and languages, and with this focus on ELF and the wider GEs paradigm comes more potential for considering this link. Much discussion in ELF and GEs relates to debates surrounding whose language (specifically, whose English) should be taught and learned. As has traditionally been the case, should the teaching and learning of English observe native speaker norms and benchmarks? Alternatively, should pedagogical approaches and materials instead recognise and celebrate the inevitable diversity in the way that English is used around the world? Parallel to this argument, Jooste and Heleta raise the question of 'whose values and norms will guide global citizens?' (2017: 44). They argue that in conceptualisations and enactments of global citizenship, there has been a strong tendency towards drawing on Western understandings of citizenship, which are often focused on the role of the individual, which they believe likely have limited applicability to numerous societies around the world that tend to organise themselves more according to communal principles:

> Disregard for non-Western values, norms, and standards by the global citizenship movement should not come as a surprise as the advocates of cosmopolitanism and global citizenship have in the past only "embraced and advocated . . . Western liberal democratic values at the expense of non-Western values" (Bowden, 2003, p. 360). Calhoun (2003) argues that despite their claims, cosmopolitans and global citizens are not "culture free; they do not simply reflect the rational obligations of humanity in the abstract" (p. 543). . . . Continuing to project "Western values and interests as global and universal which naturalises the myth of Western

supremacy in the rest of the world" (Andreotti, 2006, p. 44) will only lead to further distancing of the North and South. (Ibid.)

It is clear the various lines of argumentation that emerge from their contentions about global citizenship that are consistent with common debates in the field of English language education: issues relating to the dominance of Western values, erroneous claims about cultural neutrality and a failure to engage with charges of imperialist impositions. Furthermore, the important role that English language proficiency plays in commonly held views about what it means to be a global citizen, and how this leads to many people without access to English being excluded from global citizenship, is also pertinent here (see Henderson 2013: 5). It is precisely these concerns that the GEs paradigm seeks to address.

While much of the focus in the field of GEs and ELF has necessarily been on non-native speakers of English – (to the extent that ELF was originally conceptualised as taking place *only* between non-native speakers; it excluded native speakers – this original view tends to no longer be upheld, rather it is accepted that ELF communication can encapsulate non-native and native speakers alike – see Jenkins, Cogo and Dewey 2011) – it is also important to pose the question about the extent to which native speakers' linguistic identity may be impacted by non-native speakers deploying the language as a means of expressing a cosmopolitan identity and sense of citizenship. Primarily, it brings into question the issue of ownership of the language, which until recently was largely uncontested (i.e. a language belongs to its native speakers). Given that nowadays the number of non-native speakers of English far outweighs the number of native speakers, ownership has become a complex issue. Furthermore, with increased awareness and codification of different varieties of Englishes (which started with the World Englishes movement in the 1980s, for example with the introduction of Kachru's three circles model, e.g. Kachru 1986), there is greater legitimation than ever of the plurality with which the language is used, in ways which do not adhere to native speaker norms. This way of conceptualising English has also brought into question the often-held assumption that the responsibility for achieving successful communication lies solely with non-native speakers, rather than native speakers shouldering any of this burden (see Kubota 2001, for a report of an intervention study with native English-speaking secondary school students, which seeks to challenge this notion). Finally, for anyone who has learned English as a second language, there is the clear implication that they also have, of course, a first language. This gives them a clear advantage as multilinguals, compared to their native English-speaking counterparts, who may speak the global language but not anything else (see Lanvers 2012, for a discussion of this phenomenon).

## CRITICAL PEDAGOGIES

The final section of this chapter continues with issues already raised earlier relating to power, and crucially imbalances of power, in the conceptualisation of cosmopolitan and global citizenship, and, indeed, how these may be redressed through pedagogical choices. Engaging with power structures in the classroom has been referred to frequently as the field of 'critical pedagogies', which Darvin and Norton define as follows, with specific relation to language education:

> Educators interested in identity, language learning, and critical pedagogies are interested in language as a social practice and the way language constructs and is constructed by a wide variety of social relationships. . . . What makes the educators "critical" is the shared assumption that social relationships are seldom constituted on equal terms, reflecting and constituting inequitable relations of power in the wider society. Further, the plural use of "pedagogies" suggests that there are many ways in which pedagogy can be critical; the challenge for critical language educators is to determine how best to pursue a project of possibility for language learners, across time and diverse spaces. (Darvin and Norton 2016: 2).

Within the critical pedagogies paradigm, Darvin and Norton state that they understand language 'not only as a linguistic system but also as a social practice in which experiences are organized and identities negotiated' (ibid.). Such an understanding of language is fundamental to the argument about languages, and language education, as being a crucial tenet of citizenship: it is through language that citizenship is negotiated and enacted. Porto, Houghton and Byram (2017) outline the ways in which 'intercultural citizenship in the language classroom' may be achieved; they consider this pedagogical approach existing at the nexus between 'foreign language teaching which includes teaching for intercultural communicative competence' and citizenship education. What is necessary, they say, is:

- criticality/critical cultural awareness
- a focus on 'others' who live beyond our national boundaries and speak another language
- comparative analysis of our own situation and theirs. (Adapted from Porto, Houghton and Byram 2017: 3)

What has often been discussed, in terms of seeking to define different conceptualisations of the role education plays in establishing citizenship, is the space given to one's engagement with their own culture. In an interview conducted by Porto (2013) with Byram, the latter explains his position on the following, namely, that how we interact with our own culture is at the heart of the difference between education for citizenship and education for cosmopolitan citizenship:

> Personally I think that cosmopolitan citizenship, which implies that you give up any attachment to your national identity and see yourself as a citizen of the world, even if desirable, is not practical. . . . But the problem about education for citizenship, as it's normally done, is that it only focuses upon the nation. I'm not saying that we should suppress national identity by any means, but what foreign language teachers (and others if they wish) can contribute to, is to extend the perspective to the international, and to find ways (it's not easy) in which

> an international perspective, and an international identification, can be created through cooperating and working with people of another country. . . . I'm not so sure that . . . there can be such a thing as cosmopolitan citizenship . . . where you have only an identification with the global society or the global village. Personally I don't think there can. But international citizenship – a sense of identification with people of other national identifications – is possible. . . . What we're trying to do is move beyond the national borders and the restrictions in thinking that that creates into some kind of international citizenship rather than cosmopolitan citizenship. (Porto 2013: 153–154)

Ultimately, his point is about the value of retaining and developing multiple perspectives, identities and citizenship, and that this can be done through educational means. In this interview, Byram also makes clear what he perceives to be the link between critical pedagogies and citizenship education: it is part of the remit of education to foster in students not only a 'critical perspective, but also a willingness to take action'. This element of participation is where he sees the nexus between the two to lie (Porto 2013: 153).

While Byram focuses much of his discussion on language teaching and learning, and the role of critical pedagogies and citizenship education within this, he also makes clear that considerations of language are pertinent even in other subject areas: subject matter in any area of the curriculum is, necessarily, taught, learned and explored through a linguistic medium (Porto 2013: 147). A recent example of empirical work which supports this idea is Pitts and Brooks (2017). Their work looks at critical pedagogies within the broad context of the internationalisation of higher education, and more specifically how critical pedagogies may be used to foster global learning and global citizenship among students in different geographic locations, and societal and cultural contexts, communicating within what they call a 'third space', that is to say, a learning setting which belongs simultaneously to nobody and everybody (Pitts and Brooks 2017: 254). In their critical discourse analysis approach to exploring students' interaction in a global learning environment, they explain the importance of language in developing critical pedagogies for global citizenship education:

> Language is . . . the site through which students can wrangle with, negotiate, and examine cultural relations. Engagement in and reflection on their own discourse can provide a means for illuminating points of oppression, can reveal how particular hierarchies are claimed and maintained, and also opens up the possibilities for transformation as promised by proponents of third space philosophies. (Pitts and Brooks 2017: 257)

This example highlights a belief in the benefits students may reap from a critical pedagogies approach. However, further reflection from Byram warns us of the complexity in its implementation. He and Porto engage in a debate about the extent to which introducing such an approach is tantamount to establishing an 'agenda', or making clear a certain ideology, with the (implicit or explicit) implication being that other ideologies are therefore unwelcome, or even wrong (Porto 2013: 149). Byram is keen to clarify that he does not believe criticality in education to be an 'agenda', but rather a 'perspective' (ibid.). However, when Porto challenges him on the extent to which it could be perceived as such in societal and educational contexts where raising questions (that is to say, a fundamental tenet of criticality) is not the norm (the examples they cover are China and Japan), he concedes that there perhaps then is a 'moral agenda' (Porto 2013: 152).

Theoretical work from Andreotti (e.g. 2006) in the field of global citizenship education also touches on these conceptual difficulties. She outlines her beliefs about the differences between 'soft' and 'critical' global citizenship education, the latter being a way of facilitating individuals engaging in a probing and questioning way to understand in more depth issues relating to inequalities at a global level; the former relates more to simply raising awareness of such processes. For example, in terms of the ultimate aim of global citizenship education, the 'soft' form enables students to engage in action, from their own familiar context or perspective; the 'critical' form, in contrast, encourages students to think deeply, in a critical way, about the impact of their own culture, in order to be able to make informed decisions about ethical actions that could be taken to effect change. Furthermore, she makes an important point about how vital it is for education practitioners to be 'critically literate' so as to be able to guide their students through this critical, questioning process, for if they do not have this training they may end up reinforcing the very existing structures that the pedagogy seeks to bring into question (Andreotti 2006: 49–50). However, despite Andreotti's recognisable efforts to avoid at any point dictating a specific direction that this kind of pedagogy should take, it is worth keeping in mind the debate held by Porto and Byram, discussed above, that in making any pedagogical recommendation you are indeed taking a stance about what *should* and *should not* be done in the classroom. Andreotti's outlining of the key tenets of critical global citizenships rests on an underlying belief in the importance of questioning; as noted earlier in this section, Byram admits that to some degree this is a 'moral agenda', and that it may well be easier to implement in certain educational contexts than others.

## CONCLUDING REMARKS

In this chapter, our primary intention has been to revisit for consideration and debate the complex notions of citizenship beyond the national level, and arguments for and against these conceptualisations. Moreover, we have made further strides in our linkage of citizenship and language issues by reflecting on the particular case of English usage around the world, and how this may relate to citizenship. Much of this discussion has been supported by references to criticality (e.g. critical pedagogies and critical thinking); it is here that we would like to focus our attentions in bringing this chapter to a close. As educators ourselves, our teaching work (at secondary as much as at tertiary level) has been underpinned by beliefs in the importance of developing critical thinking skills; perhaps it is fair to say this is representative of our own educational and cultural backgrounds. We are acutely aware of the potential for validity in the *agenda* argument raised towards the end, and we invite readers to think carefully about this as they process the various content and arguments put forward in this chapter. This being said, we understand the irony in asking readers to critically reflect on criticality!

**For reflection**

- Do you identify with a concept of citizenship beyond that at the national level? Why/why not?
- What are your thoughts on criticality as an 'agenda'? Is criticality problematic in certain educational contexts?

Chapter 8

# Teacher education for language and citizenship

**Objectives**

- To develop a familiarity with seminal teacher education and teacher cognition literature.
- To reflect on the applicability of the communities of practice framework for understanding teacher professional development.
- To understand the role that teacher education may play in preparing teachers to address citizenship.

## INTRODUCTION

In this chapter, we focus on the challenges and opportunities language teachers face in seeking to address citizenship within the language curriculum. The chapter aims to provide a thorough overview of the nature of theory and research surrounding second language teacher education, in order to then examine the extent to which current teacher education provision offers adequate preparation for the endeavour. Finally, the chapter covers the key aspects of the communities of practice framework, with particular reference to how it interacts with both teacher education and teacher cognition, by way of suggesting that communities of practice may offer a crucial form of in-service support for the promotion of collaboration between citizenship and language teachers. Taken as a whole, this chapter serves to provide a detailed foundation for Chapter 9, which explores issues of teaching language and citizenship in great detail.

## SECOND LANGUAGE TEACHER EDUCATION

In order to understand the extent to which mechanisms of second language teacher education (hereafter, SLTE) prepare teachers for delivering citizenship education, this section provides coverage of the field of teacher education itself, by way of contextualisation.

To offer a working definition, in a review of the field Wright (2010: 260) explained that SLTE has tended to refer in the literature to training that individuals undergo prior to embarking upon teaching practice. We will use SLTE here in a slightly broader manner, encompassing also training that may take place at any stage in a teaching career (i.e. encapsulating also periods of continuing professional development).

Wright's review of SLTE places great emphasis on the importance of reflective practice as part of the teacher training process, which represents a more bottom-up approach to SLTE in recent years, compared to more top-down approaches that had previously characterised the practice. Related to this, he argues that SLTE has become a more situated and contextualised concern, with early-career teachers being 'socialised' into the existing network of professionals: the communities of practice framework can be useful for understanding this way of conceptualising SLTE (Wright 2010: 266), and this will be dealt with in more depth later on in the chapter. He argues that the pedagogical approach in current SLTE practices tends to incorporate the following elements:

> 1. An emphasis on the student teacher's LEARNING to teach, and becoming a THINKING teacher.
> 2. This, in turn, means a great deal of REFLECTIVE ACTIVITY programmed into learning experiences, often with written records in the form of journals or diaries.
> 3. This also entails a commitment to student teacher INQUIRY – into one's own beliefs and narratives, and into the professional contexts of teaching and learning for which STs are being prepared.
> 4. It has resulted in the appropriation of pedagogies from adult education whose central idea is LEARNING FROM EXPERIENCE (Kolb 1984; Brookfield 1988, 1995; Mezirow 2000, for example). (Wright 2010: 273; emphasis in original)

The narrative approach appears to be gaining ground as a way of exploring SLTE and teacher education more generally. Narrative enquiry facilitates the understanding of the teacher training and teacher development process and, in turn, the development of teacher identity. Johnson and Golombek (2011) have explored this process, focusing in particular on the extent to which narrative enquiry can facilitate a sense of professional development in the process of SLTE. They argue that narrative enquiry enables teachers to develop a subjective understanding of their professional experiences, within a situated teaching and learning context (here we see links with Wright's points above, on considering SLTE from a perspective of socialisation). In more detail, these authors argue for the following benefits arising from narrative enquiry in SLTE: 'inquiry into experience enables teachers to act with foresight. It gives them increasing control over their thoughts and actions; grants their experiences enriched, deepened meaning; and enables them to be more thoughtful and mindful of their work' (Johnson and Golombek 2002: 6–7).

Kanno and Stuart (2011) explore these ideas relating to SLTE and empowerment throughout the training process from an identity perspective. They look at how two early-career teachers undergoing training in the United States experienced a shift in identity from learner to teacher, and how these changes in identity informed their classroom pedagogy (2011: 236–237). On the basis of this case study approach with the two novice teachers, they argue that for those at the start of their teaching career, the establishing of a strong professional identity is essential, and the implication they draw from this is that it should feature heavily in teacher education practices (ibid.). Yuan and Lee (2015) agree that identity construction should be a fundamental part of early-career training, with a parallel view to that of Kanno and Stuart that initial teacher training practices should help to build a solid sense of one's professional identity, as this being established helps teachers to be resilient when reacting to difficulties they may face in their career. On the basis of their interview, observation and diary entry data collected from three students taking part in a short-term period of teaching practice in the Chinese context, they argue specifically that: 'an integrated framework that incorporates the cognitive, social and emotional processes of identity construction could illuminate the teacher learning process and help teacher educators understand the myriads of challenges student teachers face in learning to become teachers' (Yuan and Lee 2015: 489).

Earlier work from Hennebry (2014) has raised implications specifically for MFL (Modern Foreign Languages) teacher education for European citizenship. On the basis of an interview study exploring MFL teachers' views on how they may engage with European citizenship education, she concluded (in line with Yuan and Lee's point above, relating to teacher education as a mechanism for bringing to light the difficulties faced by trainees) that SLTE should provide teachers with strategies for successfully dealing with any challenges they may face in navigating the delivery of European citizenship in the curriculum. Drawing on a document entitled 'European Profile for Language Teacher Education', she outlines that teachers should be made aware of the main tenets of the concept, and that there is scope for having European citizenship principles underpin teaching materials both in MFL and other school subjects. It is important for teachers to be provided with clear guidance in terms of specific citizenship-based content and appropriate learning objectives (Hennebry 2014: 304). Although we acknowledge the potential for integrating citizenship into a broad range of curricular areas, we intend to focus here on how it may effectively underpin language education specifically. To best understand the role that teacher education can play in preparing language teachers for the delivery of citizenship education, it is important to establish the extent to which we understand language teaching to particularly be a unique educational endeavour, compared to the teaching of other subject areas. Borg has made reference to this issue, explaining that much of the understanding of language teacher cognition has been shaped by work with areas of focus beyond that of language learning and teaching. He believes it to be an open question in the field, the extent to which teacher cognition is similar across different areas of the curriculum, arguing for the possibility of 'language awareness' to be somewhat distinct from other kinds of subject knowledge (2003: 105).

The question of the role of and perceptions about the English language, specifically, within the wider category of language teaching, brings up notable points for discussion compared to those that pertain in other curricular areas. Wright (2010:

261) touches upon the issue of English, and patterns of its learning, teaching and usage around the world, but ultimately concludes that principles of SLTE were largely overlapping, rather than being context specific. While this was done with the stated aim of seeking to make the review applicable to readers in a variety of global contexts (a laudable intention), we would contend that this overlooks some of the necessary differences that inevitably arise when learning to teach English, compared to learning to teach languages other than English (and perhaps other widely spoken languages with something of a 'global' status, such as Mandarin). Although somewhat peripheral to the issue of language teacher education, discussions from the perspective of L2 motivation (see Chapter 4 for full coverage of this topic) have outlined that there is likely a different set of considerations for English, compared to other languages, that we would argue necessarily emerge in the process of language teacher education, in terms of understanding how and why learners may engage (or disengage) from the language learning process, and what a language teacher's role may be to react to that:

> The ownership of Global English clearly does not rest with a specific geographically-defined community of speakers, especially as English is widely used as a lingua franca between speakers of other languages and not simply in interactions between so-called 'native' and 'non-native' speakers. Consequently, traditional concepts of L2 motivation such as integrativeness and attitudes to target language speakers and their culture begin to lose meaning, as there is no clear target reference group and English is seen simply as a basic educational skill not tied to a particular culture or community. (Dörnyei and Ushioda 2011: 72)

To link these points from Dörnyei and Ushioda back to the issue of teacher education specifically, Richards (2008: 3) explains that the global spread of the English language has particular implications for those entering the profession of English language teaching:

> Becoming an English language teacher means becoming part of a worldwide community of professionals with shared goals, values, discourse, and practices but one with a self-critical view of its own practices and a commitment to a transformative approach to its own role.

That there are English language teaching professionals located in a vast array of worldwide locations offers an interesting angle, one that is perhaps not shared to the same extent by teachers of other languages which do not have the same global status, or numbers of second language speakers. It raises the question about the extent to which this offers English language teachers a sense of cosmopolitan citizenship, being part of this international community. Importantly, Richards believes that being part of an international community of language teachers imbues these professionals with a certain sense of responsibility, given that it is not a 'politically or morally neutral activity' (2008: 14). That English teaching and learning specifically brings these issues to light again indicates its distinctiveness compared to the teaching and learning of other languages, which do not so readily become accused of exerting dominance and power over other languages, and their speakers, as is the case for English – a famous example of this is of course Phillipson's (e.g. 1992) discourse surrounding English as an example of 'linguistic imperialism'. In terms of the implications for SLTE, Richards proposes the following:

> Mastery of English, it is claimed, often enhances the power and control of a privileged few and in addition, English language teaching often consumes an inordinate amount of the scarce educational resources of many countries. Globalization and the spread of English raise the need for SLTE programs to engage teachers in an exploration of the political status of English in today's world, [and] the role it can play in maintaining positions of privilege and inequality. (2008: 14)

Considerations of power structures and inequality link back to Chapter 3, where we discussed how pervasive beliefs about who is a legitimate speaker of a language based on fixed notions of native speakers, and who is a legitimate citizen of a country as determined by birthplace, may lead to a sense of there being two tiers of speakers or citizens. These issues clearly pertain in the SLTE domain as well, in terms of how teacher identity is addressed in the training process. Teacher identity in this setting could either relate to professional identity, or indeed identity as a speaker of the language being taught; to both of these aspects are attached questions of competence – for example, to what extent does an individual feel competent as a teaching professional, or to what extent do they feel competent in their knowledge of the language being taught? While it may seem as though the latter would be more applicable to those who think of themselves as non-native speakers of the language they teach, it could well be the case that even individuals who teach 'their own' language, as it were, feel ill-equipped to be able to provide in-depth explanations of syntax, for example, as it is something that they have never explicitly learned (see Seidlhofer 1996; Árva and Medgyes 2000; Holliday 2006, for breadth of understanding surrounding native speaker and non-native speaker issues in language teaching). Furthermore, beliefs about citizenship in general, and one's own citizenship specifically, likely impacts on how an individual engages with and delivers citizenship curricular content. The potential for existing beliefs to influence one's teaching practice is dealt with in the next section, as are broader issues of teacher identity.

## LANGUAGE TEACHER COGNITION AND SLTE

Richards explains that there has been increasing focus on teacher cognition in SLTE, and explains that the concept: 'encompasses the mental lives of teachers, how these are formed, what they consist of, and how teachers' beliefs, thoughts and thinking processes shape their understanding of teaching and their classroom practices' (2008: 8).

He draws on Borg (e.g. 2003, 2006), a seminal name in the field of teacher cognition, who has defined it as 'what teachers know, believe and think' (2003: 81), when highlighting the potentially pivotal role for teacher cognition in teacher education, by invoking ideas relating to the teacher as a linchpin in classroom activity, and indeed the relationship between cognitive processes (e.g. beliefs) and behaviour, in this case classroom behaviour specifically. Furthermore, to link once again to issues of 'situatedness', Richards explains that 'teacher cognition is very much concerned with teachers' personal and "situated" approaches to teaching' (2008: 8).

Kubanyiova and Feryok propose some interesting points for consideration which relate to areas for improvement in better nurturing the relationship between teacher cognition and teacher education. They argue that while there are increasing strides being made in understanding the multifaceted and complex area of teacher cognition, there is a gap in understanding how this relates to classroom practices, and that this link needs to be further researched (2015: 442); furthermore, the insight gained from progress in teacher cognition research currently seems to be rather untapped, in terms of its potential to meaningfully shape teacher education (Kubanyiova and Feryok 2015: 436).

To further explore the link between teacher cognition and SLTE, various authors have proposed the notion that content delivered in teacher education programmes may actually have to vie for acceptance alongside the strength of existing attitudes, beliefs and knowledge (e.g. Borg 2003; Wright 2010: 276). Wright explains that, on that basis, SLTE has tended to make a point of incorporating this existing cognition that individuals bring with them, and exploring the potential for those delivering the training to provide alternative toolkits/approaches (2010: 267). Borg articulates the potential strength of pre-existing beliefs of those embarking upon teacher training, and where these have likely arisen from:

> Beliefs established early on in life are resistant to change even in the face of contradictory evidence (Nisbett & Ross 1980). Such beliefs take the form of episodically stored material derived from critical incidents in individuals' personal experience (Nespor 1987), and thus teachers learn a lot about teaching through their vast experience as learners, what Lortie (1975) called their 'apprenticeship of observation'. (2003: 86)

Yuan and Lee also raise the possibility that teacher education may actually influence teacher beliefs, and particularly their perceptions of their identities, in a negative way:

> The inadequate preparation and support provided for student teachers to bridge the gap between the 'ideals' (as student and as student teachers) and the 'real world' of school and classroom (as teachers) can create tensions in their teacher identity construction, and may even cause them to quit the teaching profession (Flores and Day, 2006; Freedman and Appleman, 2008). (2015: 472)

Feryok (2010: 275) agrees that it may well be difficult to modify or encourage teachers to bring into question firmly ingrained beliefs (see also Borg 2003: 88), but that over time this can indeed be done if new pedagogical approaches and techniques that perhaps run counter to existing beliefs are revisited continually over a period of time.

Much of this discussion about the intersection between teacher cognition and teacher education appears to relate to the idea of an individual's identity shifting from that of learner to that of teacher (for explicit focus on this notion, see Kanno and Stuart 2011). Strongly rooted in a Vygotskian perspective, again understanding teacher education as 'situated practice', Warford (2011: 253) emphasises the value of acknowledging the prior learning, and beliefs, that trainee teachers bring with them to teacher education. Building on the well-known Vygotskian framework of 'zone of proximal development' (ZPD), he explains that there is a slight reconceptualisation required for understanding how the ZPD should function in the context of teacher education specifically. While it has traditionally been understood that teacher (or 'expert') scaffolding is a stage which precedes independent thinking, he argues that this should be amended for teacher education, so that initially there is a stage of independent reflection on prior knowledge and beliefs, before a stage of scaffolding guided by a teacher educator.

Kanno and Stuart (2011: 249), similarly, support the aims of teacher education research which has as a starting point a belief that trainee teachers are not at all blank canvases, and argue that an extension of this is understanding the importance of focusing also on the process of an individual's professional identity development, i.e. the journey they undertake to start to perceive themselves as a teacher, which should be incorporated as a main component into teacher education practices. An important element of this approach, they say, is the notion of teacher learning as a key concept within teacher education, and how one moves from seeing themselves as a learner to seeing themselves as a teacher. Yuan and Lee (2015) parallel this stance, by claiming that implications of their study include the problematic nature of seeking to falsely disentangle language learning from SLTE – the learning and teaching of languages, they find, are inextricably bound, and to overlook this interconnectivity could hinder the development of a novice teacher's professional identity. It is here that we may well be reminded of the uniqueness of language teaching specifically, in terms of the development of a teacher's professional identity: as we have posited above, one pervasive issue in language teaching remains the question of comparing and contrasting the experiences of those who are native speakers of the language they teach with those who are non-native speakers. Richards (2008: 9) sets out the possible differences in teacher identity development, commenting that on the one hand, native speaking teachers are often afforded an identity as an authority on that language, even if they are not qualified to as high a level as their non-native speaking colleagues; on the other hand, some non-native speaking teachers may well have 'feelings of anxiety and inadequacy' (ibid.) when they compare themselves to native speaker standards.

It is also worth remembering that teacher *educators* could also helpfully be conceptualised as learners. Wright raises this issue towards the end of his review of SLTE research, arguing that continuing education for teacher educators is also a valuable line of enquiry, to ensure best practice, and indeed reflexive and innovative practice, on the part of these professionals as well:

> Their pivotal role in SLTE pedagogy and practice is, however, largely unexplored or even acknowledged. Trials and explorations of new pedagogies are almost entirely within their remit, and their role in the process is central. In the same way that classroom innovation is in the hands of teachers, so it is for teacher educators in SLTE programmes. (2010: 287)

Golombek and Doran (2014) explored the emotional aspect of undergoing the process of teacher training through journal entries from a novice teacher, which were responded to by a teacher educator. In line with comments above by Wright, Golombek and Doran also claim that:

> we as teacher educators can hold ourselves accountable by interrogating our intentions and mediational practices, and attuning them when necessary. The iterative nature of writing and responding to reflection journals enables, even compels, teacher educators to engage in their own processes of self-reflection. (2014: 110)

Finally, Borg has also made the point that teacher education can and should be helpfully informed by the findings from the field of teacher cognition research, ensuring that teacher educators have the opportunity to access the output from this field to be able to draw on an evidence base for their work with trainee teachers (Borg 2003: 106).

## THE SOCIAL ASPECT OF TEACHER EDUCATION AND TEACHER COGNITION: TEACHING AS A COMMUNITY OF PRACTICE

The final section of this chapter will consider how a communities of practice framework (e.g. Wenger 1998) could help to conceptualise approaches to in-service support that would facilitate interdisciplinary collaboration between citizenship and language teachers.

To this end, we will start by exploring the role that communities of practice have played in existing theoretical and empirical work on teacher cognition and teacher education, by drawing on the following quote from Richards, on how we might understand the practice of teaching from a teacher cognition perspective:

> From the perspective of teacher cognition, teaching is not simply the application of knowledge and learned skills. It is viewed as a much more complex cognitively-driven process affected by the classroom context, the teachers [sic] general and specific instructional goals, the learners' motivations and reactions to the lesson, the teachers' management of critical moments during a lesson. At the same time teaching reflects the teacher's personal response to such issues, hence teacher cognition is very much concerned with teachers' personal and "situated" approaches to teaching. (2008: 8)

It would appear, then, that teaching is necessarily a hugely complex practice, influenced by factors both internal and external to teachers and learners. Borg (2003: 94) contends that these myriad factors can be as varied as 'parents, principals' requirements, the school, society, curriculum mandates, classroom and school layout, school policies, colleagues, standardised tests and the availability of resources', and furthermore points out that empirical literature in this field has indicated that the pressure exerted by these stakeholders and situational issues may impede educators' capacity for implementing classroom practices that are in line with what they believe would be optimal. This is an example of where tensions may arise between teacher cognition and actual teacher practice.

There is a body of research that has sought to understand teachers' mechanisms for dealing with this challenging practice by thinking about the school, and specifically the professional network of teacher colleagues, as a community of practice. With relation to SLTE, Richards himself goes on to explain that 'in an SLTE program a teacher-learner's identity is remade through the acquisition of new modes of discourse and new roles' (2008: 9). Fundamental to this idea is the notion of individuals being 'socialised' into a new community of practice, through the process of developing a professional identity as a teacher in the teaching and learning context. This stance has framed Yuan and Lee's (2015: 471) study of pre-service teacher identity – in fact, they argue that this socialisation process extends beyond merely the period of formal training, but can take place before and after it as well. While this may well be a career-long journey, they nonetheless argue for the relevance of incorporating an understanding of wider processes of socialisation into teacher education:

> Teacher educators could . . . be more aware of the social dimension of identity construction by looking at the sites of teacher learning beyond university-based teacher development activities to incorporate various social and professional networks, such as book clubs (Kooy 2006) and online discussion forums (Sutherland, Howard, and Markauskaite 2010) into their curriculum. (Yuan and Lee 2015: 489)

An example of empirical work which has explored language teacher colleagues from a communities of practice perspective is Vaughan (2007), who investigated shared discourses among English teaching colleagues in both Mexico and Ireland, and specifically, 'how membership is realised in language' (Vaughan 2007: 173). She is particularly interested in looking at what she calls 'backstage' discourse, which is to say, the language that teachers use among themselves, which is guided by established group norms. Commenting on the way that language use helps facilitate a shared sense of membership, with specific reference to discussions on the topic of appraising students, she says:

> although the language used in the meetings to evaluate seems limited and unhelpfully non-specific, clearly, its relative simplicity belies the rather complex nature

> of the shared professional knowledge that is invoked. Only a full member of both the local and global CofP can navigate this discourse and collaborate in its construction. (2007: 182)

In the way that Yuan and Lee argued for there being more of an acknowledgement of socialisation processes in teacher education, Vaughan makes the point that the implications from her understanding of the two language-teaching workplaces as communities of practice leads to the implication that the reality of teacher discourses and practices – rather than idealised notions of how teachers work and interact – should underpin SLTE content: what teachers 'do', rather than what they 'should do' (Vaughan 2007: 186).

In terms of how this relates to language and citizenship education specifically, Hennebry has outlined elsewhere (2014) how establishing communities of practice could be a way of providing ongoing support for interdisciplinary activity between citizenship and language teachers. Through developing professional connections in this way, there is scope for teachers to be able to critically consider classroom-based problems that they may wish to improve upon, with the help of peers. It is important to emphasise how this could manifest in language teaching settings specifically, as this has not garnered as much focus as its application in other subject areas (Hennebry 2014: 304). We propose that close-knit professional networks comprising language specialists and citizenship specialists would enable successful exploitation of links between the two subject areas in a number of potentially enriching ways for students, which sit at the nexus of the two content domains. This interconnectivity has already been considered in Chapter 3, and key areas where there is substantial potential for crossover include: identity issues as they pertain to both language learning and citizenship; how understanding one's own (linguistic or citizenship) identity offers a strong foundation for then being able to engage with others; engaging positively with notions of multiplicity, and developing a detailed understanding of multiple (linguistic or citizenship) perspectives, precluding a sense of fear in such variation; and, related to this, an openness in terms of how both citizenship and language practices/competencies may be conceptualised and realised.

## SLTE, LANGUAGE AND CITIZENSHIP – A SUMMARY

Throughout this chapter we have outlined seminal work in second language teacher education and cognition, in order to raise awareness of how teachers' beliefs, and the training they undergo, are relevant for understanding how interdisciplinary links between the two (closely interrelated) subject areas may be best nurtured. We argue that establishing professional networks (conceptualised as communities of practice) may have rich potential for facilitating this crossover. Underpinning this discussion at various junctures has been a development of core issues relating to teacher (professional/linguistic/citizenship) identity, and critically reflected-on complexities within this domain. Chapter 9 builds on the foundation laid here, by exploring at length teachers' classroom practice.

**For reflection**

- To what extent do you agree that SLTE should be different for teachers of English, and teachers of other languages?
- Do you think the communities of practice framework is applicable for understanding teachers' professional interaction in your context? Is it helpful for understanding how teachers may collaborate in the domain of citizenship education?

Chapter 9

# Teaching citizenship in the language classroom

The relationship between language teaching and citizenship development has been well theorised and this theorisation has been integrated into curricula, emphasised in education policy and frequently referenced in institutional discourse at the level of national government and supra-national entities. Yet, this recognition seems rarely to translate into classroom reality (Sercu et al. 2005; Hennebry 2011). Data from teachers suggests that a primary reason for this may be based on the fact that language teacher education focuses primarily if not exclusively on the teaching of language systems rather than on promoting language as a means of developing a sense of civic responsibility and participation. Thus, while language teachers support the idea that language education has an important role to play in promoting social cohesion, they lack both the pedagogical knowledge and the professional self-efficacy to address such skills and content in their teaching (Hennebry 2012).

This chapter aims to outline some of the key principles that might helpfully shape language teaching for citizenship development, and draws on a range of sources to provide ideas on how language teachers might engage in such teaching within their classrooms.

Promoting intercultural citizenship requires teachers themselves to be interculturally aware, both in terms of their own culture and identity and in terms of their intercultural competence (Sercu 2006). However, considering the heavy emphasis on student performance, language teachers seeking to go beyond teaching linguistic systems need to critically engage with language pedagogies that go beyond a heavy skills-based approach (Levine and Phipps 2012). Levine and Phipps (2012) propose that teachers adopt a critical pedagogy wherein teacher and learners deconstruct, challenge and transform the assumptions that are built into language curricula, materials and teaching practices. Holmes (2014) suggests that learners need to understand the social and communicative processes that underpin constructions of culture and identity, comprehending their own identity and culture in order to understand that of others. Adopting this critical view of language teaching challenges essentialised and nationalistic views of culture, moving away from a high culture view and favouring instead what Holmes (2014) refers to as the five C's of *context, culture, comparisons, connections and communities.* As Holmes explains, language learning is no longer about food, festivals, facts and flags but about encouraging learners to understand how their own and others' cultures permeate and shape behaviour, interactions and language choices. Culture is thus about activity, moving from a defined entity to a dynamic process, and identity is constructed, negotiated and reconstructed through communication with others. In order to enact this view of language and culture, the language classroom needs to provide opportunities for learners to recognise, challenge and move beyond cultural stereotypes, exploring the complexity of identification with one or more given culture(s), as a matter of identity or identities.

Hall, Evans and Nixon (2013) point out that the ways we project ourselves and the cultural identities we ascribe to ourselves have become more open-ended, variable and complex, such that identities may even appear as contradictory, continuously shifting and pulling individuals in different directions. Understanding this can help learners to question the assumptions they make of others' identities, so the language classroom can helpfully create opportunities for exploring the complex and multifaceted nature of identity. Activity A, adapted from Holmes (2014) allows learners to uncover and examine their own identity as a key step towards understanding the dynamic nature of identity more broadly.

**A. Exploring identities**

Ask learners to analyse their own identity to understand its complexity, discussing their understanding in pairs.

1. (i) Ask students to think about the following questions: who am I (how do I see myself)? How do I present myself to others (what identities do I portray to others, e.g. my identity as a learner, a family member, a sports player, a male/female, a young person, serious, fun, complex, etc.)? How do others see me (what identities do others give to me)? (ii) Students discuss their answers in pairs.
2. Write down a list of all the different types of identity you can think of (e.g. family, national, linguistic, social, cultural, historical, personal, professional, local, geographical, political, religious, racial, transnational/ European/cosmopolitan, ethnic, etc.).
3. Discuss your list with your partner. Are there any new identities and terms you would like to add to your list?
4. Discuss the nature of these identities and how they differ, giving examples of each.
5. Which of the following words would you use to describe the nature of your identities? Static, expansive, flowing, definite, solid, finite, singular blurry, fragmented, fluid, changing, linear, organic, fixed, bounded, multiple, unified, flexible.

In order to build the intercultural skills necessary for effective civic participation, learners need to engage in intercultural communication that entails a process of comparison and contrast between their own socially constructed world and those of the other. Opportunities for study abroad or exchange trips offer unique advantages in this regard, although for many schools and many learners such opportunities are inaccessible. In such cases online communication with speakers of other languages can provide something akin to an in-country experience, allowing learners to transition from tourist to sojourner. Lázár (2015) reports on a web collaboration project for promoting intercultural competence among learners of English as a foreign language for whom the possibility of direct face-to-face contact with speakers of other languages was limited. The key features of the project are outlined below, providing insights into ways of promoting intercultural citizenship through opportunities to develop the skills and competencies identified by Byram (1997) and Fantini (2000), already discussed in Chapter 3.

**B. The icEurope project**

**Background**

Funded by the European Lifelong Learning Comenius project entitled *icEurope- Intercultural Communication in Europe*, aiming at exploring intercultural competence development within web-enhanced English classrooms in 2010.

**Students**

Seventy-eight intermediate level, secondary school learners of English in Bulgaria, Hungary, Italy and Turkey.

**Teachers**

Four English teachers from Bulgaria, Hungary, Italy and Turkey.

**Duration**

Five months.

**Themes**

Introducing yourself; introducing your home town; meals and table manners; popular songs; reflections for future web-collaboration students.

**Preparation**

- Before the learner collaboration took place, the teachers were invited to participate in associated training and materials development. The teachers assisted the project team in developing the online teaching materials to support intercultural work with their learners.
- Themes were adapted according to local curricula.
- Students were asked to complete an initial questionnaire about their language learning history, their intercultural contacts and their computer skills. This acted as a needs analysis but also allowed the project team to observe any developments in intercultural awareness over the course of the project.

**Materials**

- Materials were primarily based on videos found on YouTube and activities adapted from the Peace Corps learning and training materials

(www.peacecorps.gov/culturematters) and the intercultural communication textbook *Mirrors and Windows* (Huber-Kriegler, Lázár and Strange 2003).
- Contact between the classes took place via the open source learning management system, Moodle.
- The Moodle site hosted discussion forums, journals, wikis, assignments and two live chat sessions.

**Delivery**
- Learners worked together via Moodle in discussing and reflecting on a variety of topics related to the project themes.
- Learners spent one lesson a week of class time on the project, with teacher guidance, and were also grouped into four mixed, international teams of approximately twenty students, comprising four or five students from each country.
- Each teacher was in charge of one of the four international classes as well as their own class.
- The project adopted a blended learning approach, whereby in addition to the Moodle discussions students also received linguistic and cultural preparation in the classroom, allowing for authentic and purposeful intercultural communication in the foreign language when conducting the online tasks.
- 'Rich points' (Agar 1996) emerging from learners' forum posts, journal entries and wikis were integrated into subsequent topics and tasks. These were then also discussed in class allowing for deeper understanding and awareness raising. Thus, learners played a part in influencing the choice of topics and activities, helping also to construct the material used in the project (Kohn and Warth 2011).

**Main student activities**
- Introductory forum – get to know each other.
- Introductory wikis – classes present themselves to the others.
- Map it! Journal – research and learn basics about the other cities/countries.
- Mini-portfolio 1 – individuals and teams track their progress.
- Breakfast forum – discuss differences in breakfast dishes and habits.
- Dinner forum – exchange ideas about dishes and habits connected to dinner.
- Main findings wiki – summarise what has been learned.
- Culture and language journal – reflect on their culture and language learning, for team to evaluate.
- Mini portfolio 2 – individuals and team track their progress.
- Music guesses forum – guess the meaning of other students' choice of song.
- Music journal – reflect on other classes' songs and their 'cultural translation'.
- Visiting/goodbye – to discuss visits and say goodbye to their international classes.

**Assessment and evaluation**

- Final student questionnaire – to learn about students' views on their achievements.
- Two student group interviews – to collect additional data about five students' views.
- Newsletter for future students – to collect data on students' learning and evaluation.
- Teachers' journal – to collect data about teachers' views on results.
- Project management forum – to collect data about teachers' and partners' views on results.
- Lesson observations to collect data by observing the teaching-learning process

Lázár's (2015) full account of the project provides useful insights for the development of other such initiatives aimed at promoting intercultural competence while contributing to intercultural citizenship. As a first step, the activities that are mapped out in the project allow for students' verbalisation of the ethnocentric views they hold, uncovering them and making them explicit to the students themselves as they reflect on their own verbalisations. Only by opening them up in this way can learners then be made aware of the need to decentre and consider other perspectives. This is a key step in any form of intercultural education. Secondly, the project highlights the importance of understanding intercultural competence development as a process that takes time. Lázár (2015) reports that it was only after more than two months of the project that the first real interactions appeared in the student forums. He suggests that this may have been the result of teachers prompting students to reflect on what constitutes rich and respectful discussion, as well as being due to a growing sense of group membership, consolidating the members' trust as time elapsed. Thirdly, while the topics covered in the project are suggestive of a 'Products, Practices and Perspectives' view of culture, akin with high culture, the dialogic processes the learners engaged in offer opportunities for promoting Byram's *savoir faire* and *savoir être*, the know-hows, through developing the skills of comparison and critical cultural relativism. Fourthly, teachers' interventions at critical moments, whether in preparing for activities, debriefing activities or adapting activities in response to observations, allow for maximising the potential benefits of the experience, reflecting observations by Schartner (2016) and Behrnd and Porzelt (2012) that cultural exposure should be accompanied by conscious pedagogical efforts. The fifth and final consideration is to ensure that the project provides opportunities for authentic and rich language use and language exposure. One example cited by Lázár (2015) was the music guessing game. Students shared their songs and had to guess the meaning or the message of the songs chosen by other classes. They were subsequently asked to provide translations of the songs which went beyond simply a good language translation, looking instead for a translation that explained any possible unfamiliar cultural references or connotations, requiring them not only to decentre and predict what cultural aspects might cause confusion for their counterparts, but also to engage with linguistic nuances and subtleties. The project enables learning goals to 'shift from memorizing facts to exploring learners' own cultures, discovering culture as context and its impact on human behaviour and communication, learning about universal, culture-general phenomena and culture-specific information about one particular culture, as well as learning how to learn' (Lázár 2015: 218).

Other important learner outcomes referred to were a sense of achievement in communicating effectively, putting language learning to good use, experiencing the ability to communicate in real life in the foreign language, as well as positive feelings about having real contact with real people. The nature of school learning is such that language teachers often resort to motivating learners by talking about a future when one day they will be able to use the language they have learned for real purposes. These experiences mentioned above can give students a foretaste of that future. One of the key merits of initiatives such as the icEurope project is that they offer students real-time opportunities to engage in meaningful dialogue with speakers of other languages, making language learning purposeful and truly authentic.

Trejo and Fay (2013) describe another example of using online learning for promoting core intercultural citizenship skills. The project was conducted in Mexico and in the context of what the authors termed an English as a foreign language rather than an ELF approach to the target language. The project sought to enrich the existing provision through extra-curricular development of an intercultural approach coherent with the ELF curriculum aims, and shifting towards awareness raising of general cultural variations students might experience through their ELF-based intercultural encounters. The authors used the term General Cultural Awareness (GCA), seeking to enable students to adopt a 'spirit of non-judgmental openness and curiosity' and to begin developing the habit of 'anticipating both expected and unexpected similarities and differences (in cultural values, beliefs, practices, activities, products, and so on)' (Trejo 2010: 31).

**C. Wiki-based critical incidents project**

**Students**

University students aged 19–22 years, taking lower-intermediate English as a foreign language class in the language centre of a Mexican university.
Students are grouped into trios or pairs.

**Design**

The design of the project was based around the use of critical incidents (CIs) as focus points around which to base students' individual and collaborative intracultural engagement. The CIs presented intercultural encounters in which effective communication was undermined by misunderstandings resulting from participants' ethnocentric habit of mind as they interpreted the values and behaviours of others. The project was planned in three phases, which are outlined below.

**Delivery**

The project uses wikis, a Web 2.0 tool that allows continuous and easy modifications to loosely structured webpages that can link to each other and to other internet resources. The use of wikis enables students to collaborate as they disseminate information and exchange and discuss ideas.

***Phase 1***

Face-to-face introductions to the wiki and how to use it.

***Phase 2***

Wiki-based introductions by the group members, as they did not previously know each other.

***Phase 3***

*CI-based project activities*

Each group is given a CI. The CIs across the group were all different, providing a range of experiences of intercultural encounters and of communication challenges. Based on the CIs, there are seven key tasks for students to engage with:

1. Individual students read the CI and post their initial reaction on the wiki. They include speculations about other possible explanations and engage in web-based discussion about the different interpretations.

2. Building on discussions, each group brainstorms areas of research that might help to develop more informed responses to their particular CI.

3. Each student undertakes an area of research and posts their findings onto their group's wiki page. They revisit their initial reaction to the CI on the basis of their findings and engage in further discussion of their collectively-informed interpretations.

4. Moving from a within-group stage to a between-group stage, each group invites the other groups to engage with their CI via their wiki, such that all students encounter all CIs. Having developed possible explanations for their own CI, students now offer responses on the new CIs and engage in discussion, sharing the results of their research with the other students.

5. Students are able to 'eavesdrop' online on the developing thinking of the other groups as they engage with the new CIs.

6. Each group consolidates their thinking about the various CI interpretations through means of a presentation to the other groups.

7. Students explore how the issues raised might play out in their home context, noting similarities and challenging monolithic interpretative stances.

The wiki-based project sought to enrich existing language provision by including an intercultural element, in order to raise students' general cultural awareness and cultural engagement skills. It was all underpinned by the desire to shift towards a general cultural awareness rather than one tied to a specific target culture.

A cognitive approach to intercultural learning was adopted, which rejected the idea of intercultural learning as transmission of cultural information. Instead, through discussion from multi-perspectives, students engaged with intercultural stimuli. The project aimed at changing 'habits of the mind' (Mezirow 2000: 17), promoting intellectual empathy, considered as a necessary 'trait of mind necessary to fair-mindedness' involving the 'awareness of the need to imaginatively put oneself in the place of others so as to genuinely understand them' (Paul and Elder 2002: 26).

In order to evaluate the project, the researchers examined data from a student questionnaire, in addition to the project wiki pages, to then conduct stimulated recall with a small group of students, looking particularly for evidence of curiosity, openness to different interpretations of the CIs, and the development of the habit of anticipating expected and unexpected cultural similarities and differences. While a detailed account of the evidence is presented in Trejo and Fay (2013), the data suggested that the project was successful in beginning to develop in students a new habit of mind tending towards openness and curiosity in the face of otherness. The researchers describe the project aims as modest, but the development of openness and curiosity in the face of otherness is recognised as being central to shaping the necessary attitudes for effective intercultural citizenship. It is precisely this last stance that enables the individual to engage with rather than avoid diversity and to work towards building bridges between the familiar and the unfamiliar.

**D. Autobiography of Intercultural Encounters (AIE)**
**Materials**

The AIE package comprises the following:

- The autobiography of intercultural encounters
  *The autobiography takes the learners through a series of steps*
- The autobiography of intercultural encounters for younger learners.
- Notes for facilitators.
- Context, concepts and theories
  *A concept paper outlining the context, concepts and theories that underpin the autobiography*
- Concepts for discussion
  *A modified version of the concept paper for use in discussion and debate with older students*

An autobiography of intercultural encounters through visual media has also been developed in recognition of the significant impact that images have on the way we understand the world around us. This version seeks to promote students' critical thinking of the ways in which images are used to construct the world for us.

In the case of Europe, the AIE was developed in response to the recommendations made in the Council of Europe's White Paper on Intercultural Dialogue 'Living Together as Equals in Dignity' (http://www.coe.int/dialogue), calling specifically for the development of tools that would encourage students to exercise 'independent critical faculties including to reflect critically on their own response and attitudes to experiences of other cultures' (para. 152). The resource is developed by Michael Byram and his colleagues and underpinned by Byram's work on intercultural communicative competence.

Through engaging individuals with a series of reflective questions about a particular intercultural encounter which has been of special significance, the AIE seeks to encourage the development of the skills and intercultural competences required for richer communication and deeper understanding across national divides.

The AIE, which was developed in conjunction with the Council of Europe (2009), has been widely recognised as a useful tool for developing learners' awareness of self in relation to others, reflecting on both the differences and similarities between themselves and their interlocutors and inviting them to consider what actions may result from each particular encounter.

The 'Contexts, Concepts and Theories' document provides an overview of the key concepts relating to intercultural communication, which is a particularly useful resource for teachers venturing into this area who have had little prior exposure to these ideas in their own teacher education. Similarly, the 'Concepts for Discussion' document supports teachers in introducing language learners to these important concepts, thus enabling deeper reflection on the issues entailed in intercultural encounters.

Projects described in the literature focus on the development of intercultural skills and attitudes, which are an essential cornerstone in the development of intercultural citizens. A further important aspect to consider is a sense of civic responsibility to one's immediate community and beyond, coupled with a desire to meaningfully contribute to the flourishing of society. To this end, projects that engage students with civic action through the means of their language learning provide an opportunity to experience the ways in which language learning can be the means through which to enact meaningful local, national and cosmopolitan citizenship. Some examples of ways in which this might be brought into practice are presented below:

## EXAMPLE 1: SECONDARY-PRIMARY SCHOOL COLLABORATION FOR CIVIC RESPONSIBILITY

Collaborations between primary and secondary schools can facilitate opportunities for language learners to teach the language they have learned to younger learners with less linguistic competence. In addition to the wide range of psychosocial benefits that such activities can offer to both the student tutors and tutees, teaching the language to others can enhance student tutors' language self-efficacy, while it may also encourage metacognition in their own language learning, promoting systematic approaches to language learning and inspiring creativity in language learning.

## EXAMPLE 2: CROSS-CULTURAL COLLABORATION FOR CIVIC RESPONSIBILITY

Many language curricula include units on introducing one's own town or city. Teachers can encourage students to go beyond physical descriptions, to describe the social structures in their towns, the opportunities for youth, the kinds of community projects that are necessary to the social and economic needs of each group, the different demographic groups that live in the city, and the kinds of job opportunities that exist and that the majority of the members of the community take up. Developing these descriptions is both an opportunity for rich language use and for developing an understanding of the world in which they live and the opportunities and needs of their community. Reflecting features of the supra-national regional icEurope project, for example, schools can establish partnerships across countries or cultural contexts such that students can engage in dialogue about their communities' opportunities and needs, also generating ideas for how best to contribute meaningfully either to their own respective community or to each other's communities. For instance, this might be through collaborative fundraising for specific causes, through collecting books, toys, clothing for the participating communities or further communities that have been identified as a focus of the project, through creating promotional materials to share with other schools, or other groups of language learners.

Projects such as this require learners, firstly, to develop an understanding of the realities of the world in which they live and operate, beyond their own community; secondly, to understand the needs of their fellow human beings whatever their background; thirdly, to collaborate with diverse individuals for meaningful purposes; and, fourthly, to use each language in a purposeful, meaningful and authentic way, generating strategies for enhancing communication where language proficiency may be lacking in strength. The experience of using the foreign language in a joint endeavour towards a shared goal can be a powerful means of demonstrating to learners the ways in which linguistic competence enables processes and outcomes that otherwise might not be possible and of generating great satisfaction in language learning.

Such initiatives require careful planning and commitment but have the potential to enrich the language learning experience, making it more meaningful and authentic, both for the learner and for the teacher. Language is the primary means through which we build relationships, express and enact our identities, realise our aspirations and eventually bring about social change. In the multilingual world that learners and teachers inhabit today, language teaching in many contexts is impoverished through a focus only on form, with little attention given to the role that language plays in all the other aspects of life. With commitment and creativity, teaching practitioners have the possibility to change that.

## EXAMPLE 3: SERVICE LEARNING FOR CIVIC RESPONSIBILITY

A helpfully detailed discussion of Intercultural Service Learning (ISL) is provided by Rauschert and Byram (2018), and we would like to offer an overview here, pointing to its usefulness for promoting intercultural citizenship. Rauschert and Byram (2018) propose that a combination of Service Learning and intercultural citizenship education integrated into language teaching has the potential for a complementarity that uniquely enriches the learning experience. Service Learning refers to an educational approach combining formal learning with community service, connecting curricular, course-based learning and service activity. Minor defines Service Learning as:

> [. . .] a union of community service and formal learning. It involves students going into their communities and using what they learn in class to help people, and then bringing what they learn in their community back into the classroom to enhance their academic learning. It is service with learning objectives and learning with service objectives. (2001: 10)

Other definitions are available (e.g. Bringle and Hatcher 1995; Speck and Hoppe 2004), but the core principle of Service Learning is that the service component is integral to the teaching and learning process rather than an additional extra or an extra-curricular activity, such that community service that is not developed in collaboration with an institution of education would not be defined as Service Learning. Service Learning then has the dual function of enhancing students' academic curriculum and helping foster civic responsibility (United States Congress 1990: 5).

The beginnings of Service Learning can be traced back to North America at the beginning of the twentieth century, with proponents such as John Dewey, who argued that schools should not only teach knowledge but also include aspects of citizenship education and foster a 'spirit of service'. At the heart of Service Learning is the notion of promoting 'strong' or 'creative democracy' (Dewey 1916, 1938; Barber 1984), encouraging citizens to contribute meaningfully to society. Bringing together a pragmatic and idealistic notion of education, Service Learning is underpinned by an experiential learning, project-based methodology, promoting the view that 'knowledge is always an active attempt to respond to one's situation in the world' (Rocheleau 2004: 4). Since the 1980s, Service Learning has expanded rapidly, particularly in the United States.

The methodological framework offered by Service Learning enables the coupling of formal learning in diverse curriculum areas with project-based citizenship education. ISL is one such form that is particularly suited to language teaching, combining a focus on intercultural learning with an emphasis on civic service. In ISL, the community is broadened out from the local or national community referred to in traditional Service Learning, to the global community instead (Jacoby and associates (1996)). Nevertheless, given the nature of today's globalised world and multicultural communities the learner need not go far to engage with ISL. Rauschert and Byram (2018) talk about three types of ISL: (1) within one country: collaboration between diverse ethnic groups in the same country; (2) between countries: collaboration between people living in different countries and staying in their own country during the project; and (3) abroad: Service Learning projects that entail service during a period abroad. ISL projects a structured means of bringing ethnically, culturally or socially diverse groups of young people together to learn from one another as they share their views and experiences while serving the community (Youth Service America (YSA) 2007). As Rauschert and Byram (2018) point out, the combination of communication, intercultural learning and civic action makes ISL a valuable contribution to language teaching. Specifically, the language provides the means through which young people come together bridging diverse cultures, histories and languages to generate understanding and address issues of social significance. Thus, ISL integrated into language education fosters academic learning while contributing to sustainable development and world peace (Furco 2003; Billig 2010; Brandon and Clayton 2011; Rauschert 2014).

The effectiveness of ISL is contingent on the quality of the implementation. Four general criteria suggested by the German nationwide Service Learning network ('Lernen durch Engagement') are: (1) students should identify a real need/problem in the community; (2) projects must be linked to curricular content; (3) by taking action in the community, the students' learning also takes place outside the school; and (4) there is a high degree of reflection throughout the project (Seifert and Zentner 2010: 5). And as Rauschert and Byram (2018) highlight, the nature and depth of reflection are crucial in determining the quality of ISL projects. To this end, they propose methods such as structured debriefing, commonly used in Service Learning and entailing a cycle of reflection requiring the participant to describe what happened and the feelings they experienced during the project, as well as evaluating the experience, and analysing any value judgements, conclusions and personal action plans for future situations (see Gibbs 1988; Sliwka and Frank 2004: 54). In this way, learners develop skills of analysis and critical thinking.

There are also important considerations that must be made regarding the relationship between service providers and service recipients within the ISL project, ensuring that relationships are held to the highest ethical standard, avoiding, for instance, inadvertently fostering hierarchical structures. This needs to be ensured from the outset since ISL projects typically involve close collaboration between provider and recipient even in the planning stages. Such hierarchy can result from a sense of cultural or socio-economic disparity. ISL projects are to be developed on the basis of empathy rather than pity. Developing a view of the ISL project as a joint venture towards equal opportunities, human rights and sustainable development may require some preparatory groundwork to be done in the language classroom, encouraging students to explore any assumptions and preconceptions they may hold of other cultures generally and the partner culture specifically, as well as their understandings of the respective roles in the project and forms of communication that may foster or hinder respect and equity. High-quality Service Learning should be underpinned and accompanied by structured reflection, performed on the basis of theoretical frameworks.

ISL shares common goals with intercultural citizenship education (ICE), as both seek to: (1) foster intercultural competence; and (2) stimulate critical thinking and action in the community. ICE arguably places greater emphasis on developing criticality (Porto and Byram 2015), while a primary concern in ISL is the promotion of civic responsibility to the community, whether local, national or global.

ICE has developed in recognition of the fact that effective communication requires not only the due language competences and understanding of socially appropriate uses of language, but also 'intercultural' skills and attitudes through which to understand other ways of life and thought and engage meaningfully with speakers of other languages and their ways of living and thinking. An important aspect of ICE is also the ability to consciously reflect both on one's own and on others' values, beliefs and way of life (Byram 1997), critically examining the basis on which cultural analysis and evaluation is generated, as was discussed in Chapter 1, examining the competencies that Byram outlined as central to the development of the intercultural citizen.

Of particular relevance to discussions of ISL is the inclusion of community involvement in the form of the 'savoir s'engager' (Byram 2008). Community in the context of ICE and seen through the language education lens can once again refer to culturally diverse local communities, but also to the global community beyond the local confines. Through the integration of ICE, ISL and language teaching, learners are encouraged to broaden their concept of community and involvement if they are allowed to use their foreign-language skills to interact with citizens of other countries.

The integration of service to the community was a response to influence from citizenship education (Byram 2008). Byram et al. (2017) report on a study implementing this model through a network of teachers and their classes who engaged in interactions across the internet, identifying a topic of common interest, analysing it from international perspectives, and then engaging with community involvement around the concept.

Analysing participants' reflections in an implementation of the Autobiography of Intercultural Encounters, Porto (2014) reports on the impact of participating in an ICE project. Evaluation of ICE typically entails the analysis of data gathered during the implementation, such as students' interactions across the internet, their self-analyses and reports, followed by an examination of the data in light of the intended aims of developing criticality, an international identification and perspective, and the impact on language acquisition. Yet, there is little systematic understanding of the impact of ICE, and the development of clear criteria for its evaluation will be crucial for its adoption more extensively in curricula across contexts and education frameworks. The criteria developed in ISL may prove a useful starting point in this endeavour.

Rauschert and Byram (2018) argue that despite the different origins of the two approaches, the extensive overlap between ICE and ISL presents potential for productive synergy based on sharing theoretical considerations and best practices. They point out that the established nature of ISL and the substantial body of research that accompanies it provide a useful framework for developing evaluation research on ICE and a point of comparison for understanding its impact. Furthermore, this possible synergy would offer enrichment opportunities for developing appropriate and effective pedagogies. The successful implementation of ISL in language teaching requires drawing on the theoretical foundations and clearly defined objectives of ICE, particularly in relation to critical cultural awareness. The possibility of collaborating within an internationally diverse group sharing a service focus and objective has powerful potential to promote in students a sense of the intercultural cosmopolitan citizen who can benefit from participation in intercultural relations, but also motivates them to make a meaningful social contribution as part of this process.

Seeking to support teachers in integrating citizenship in language teaching, this chapter proposes a range of activities and approaches that can provide a means of promoting skills and attitudes pertaining to cosmopolitan citizenship. It highlights the potential for ISL in encouraging language learners towards social participation and enacting civic responsibility through their language learning experiences.

Chapter 10

# Drawing implications for policy and practice

This volume aims to provide an overview of some of the available examples of relationships between language learning and citizenship education, within the multifaceted and rapidly increasing connectivity that characterises the global community at the present time.

Language learning in its fullest sense has never been simply set of systems and rules, it has always been a form of trying to express through language the deepest essence of diverse human groups, forging relationships and bonds between individuals, communities and cultures. This is no less true today amidst the challenges that threaten to alienate social groups from one another, contrasting at the same time with the unprecedented technological opportunities for reaching out beyond local and national borders. In the context of these challenges and opportunities, active civic participation is fundamental to strengthening the fabric of society promoting cohesion and collaboration. Language education and language teachers are placed centre stage in the mission to prepare students to maintain and be able to contribute with their own richness to the pluralistic, multilingual and multicultural global environment of today. To this end, language learners require more than ever the attitudes and skills of consideration of the otherness; the curiosity to ask questions about the unfamiliar in the endeavour to understand it and not to pre-conceive it; an appreciation for other ways of life; a willingness to self-reflect and critically examine their own perceptions, values, assumptions; a clear sense of their own identity and values, from which they can have the confidence to appreciate those of others; a sense of responsibility as an intercultural citizen; and a desire to fulfil those responsibilities in society in different ways, for the flourishing of individuals and the communities.

## IMPLICATIONS FOR TEACHER EDUCATION

A majority of language teachers appears to support the idea that language learning not only has an instrumental purpose that may well go beyond the mere learning of the rules of a particular language, but that also may embrace a deeper educative purpose (Porto, Houghton and Byram 2017). This is clear from the data presented in Chapter 6 and it is supported by a range of studies conducted in recent decades.

Convery et al. (1997), for instance, found that student teachers in the United Kingdom were in favour of incorporating a European dimension as a means of considering European citizenship. Osler (1998) found student teachers across seven European countries to be highly committed to developing learners' intercultural awareness and understanding. Sercu et al. (2005) found that teachers across Belgium, Sweden, Mexico, Spain, Greece, Poland and Bulgaria were in favour of developing learners' intercultural competence through language teaching. And yet, despite the apparent support from policy, theory, research and practitioners, in addition to the global climate of the day that clearly places the need for active intercultural citizenship centre stage, the role of language teaching appears to have remained unfulfilled in this area, with notably few concrete exceptions.

Given the realities of the classroom and the ongoing misalignment of policy with these realities, pre-service and in-service teachers need opportunities for ongoing reflective practice as a key mechanism for equipping them to work through the obstacles they are likely to face as they work towards promoting intercultural citizenship. These practitioners appear to have a basic need for allotted time, structured within the teaching schedule, dedicated to engagement in collaborative dialogue within and across curriculum areas for sharing best practice, innovating within their pedagogical approaches, and generating creative ways of integrating intercultural citizenship into their teaching practice. Beyond this basic need for time, they need support also to engage in critical reflection on the ways in which they could conceptualise and enact their own identities as intercultural citizens. For many pre- and in-service language teachers the notion of the intercultural citizen, though a lived experience, may not feature prominently in their consciousness and so opportunities for verbalising what this concept means to them, how it plays out in their everyday encounters, what their own active civic participation looks like, and so on, are crucial, though so far they do not appear to have been attended to.

There is a strong relationship between teachers' beliefs about their professional capabilities (professional self-efficacy) and teachers' classroom behaviour. Studies point to the idea that teachers' professional self-efficacy is crucial as they orient their identities as practitioners (Hammerness et al. 2005; Varghese et al. 2005).

Bandura's well-established self-efficacy theory proposed that the individual's belief in his or her own ability is a powerful drive influencing motivation to act and effort expended in a particular endeavor, and may regulate the persistence of coping mechanisms in the face of setbacks. According to Bandura (2001), levels of self-efficacy are influenced by an individual's self-assessment of his or her ability and competence to achieve a goal. A significant factor in this is likely to be the degree of relevant knowledge the individual possesses. Teachers' self-assessment of their pedagogical content knowledge relevant to the teaching of intercultural citizenship is likely to significantly influence their self-efficacy and therefore their openness to engage with such teaching.

Given the importance attributed to teachers' subject knowledge and pedagogical subject knowledge (Moats 2000; McCutchen et al. 2002a; McCutchen et al. 2002b; Wong Fillmore and Snow 2002; Phelps and Schilling 2004; Phelps 2009), teacher education that adequately prepares language teachers for the task of developing intercultural citizenship needs to be paid particular attention to, specifically with regard to these aspects, as a means of ensuring a robust professional self-efficacy among teachers based on realistic, positive self-assessment (Chacon 2005; Eslami and Fatahi 2008).

Given the obstacles and challenges language teachers are likely to face in seeking to promote awareness of intercultural citizenship, teacher education programmes need to equip teachers to take ownership of their teaching practices and develop professional autonomy that will enable them to persevere in the face of constraints, in order to enact the kind of teaching practice that aligns with their expertise and professional beliefs. The shift towards socio-cultural views of teacher learning (Crandall 2000; Johnson 2006) has seen increasing importance attributed to teacher learning and the emergence of tools such as action research for equipping teachers with systematic means of developing reflective practice *in situ* and in response to challenges and obstacles they face in the classroom, thus enhancing self-efficacy for their own development and that of their students. Practicum-based teacher education adopting such tools has a positive effect on teachers' self-efficacy (Atay 2007; Faez and Valeo 2012).

In response to case study findings suggesting that training for teaching cultural values is very rare, Kelly et al. (2004) developed the frame of reference for their regional, supra-national grouping that was in this case a European Profile for Language Teacher Education. This tool outlines helpful objectives for developing teacher education in European citizenship specifically but can also be a helpful starting point for developing teacher education for intercultural citizenship more broadly.

Suggestions include engaging teachers with the notion of European citizenship, addressing social, civil and political aspects, and integrating this theme into teaching through materials, teacher networks in language and other curricular areas, teacher exchanges and the promotion of the shared values that underpin their citizenship; eventually, these ideas might even be extended to teacher preparation for intercultural citizenship education.

Teacher educators can also play their part in promoting an ongoing dialogue among teachers and teacher educators throughout the teaching career trajectory. Teacher learning has come to be viewed as 'situated' (Johnson and Golombek 2011), calling for forms of teacher learning that practitioners can apply in changing contexts and that foster knowledge creation as a result of lived social practices (Wenger 2008). The development of professional networks plays an important role in providing teachers with backing and a critical context for reflecting on their practice. The notion of professional enquiry is widely recognised and well established, yet its application in language teaching research has received limited attention and the usefulness of tools such as action research for enhancing language teachers' practice in promoting intercultural citizenship is less well documented.

The teaching of intercultural citizenship, indeed all forms of citizenship, requires specific pedagogies, as has already been previously discussed. Osler and Starkey

(1999) reviewed a study conducted by the European Commission, across eighteen European countries, that sought to identify the features of education training and youth programme projects that could be seen to have contributed to effective political education and active citizenship. On the basis of their observations they made three key suggestions: firstly, individuals should learn how to seek out relevant information independently; secondly, projects should address not only information and rights, but also identities and feelings, as well as addressing structural inequalities; and thirdly, the most successful projects are those that provide opportunities for those involved with them to develop participatory skills.

Walkington and Wilkins (2000) conducted a comparison of primary school teachers in the United Kingdom with and without teaching abroad experience, specifically focusing on the pedagogies they used for citizenship development. They found that while both groups delivered the geography curriculum objectives, those with teaching abroad experience integrated the development of cosmopolitan citizenship education aims. These teachers also adopted a process-oriented pedagogy enabling the development of critical thinking skills and personal growth through participatory pedagogy. Teachers with no experience of teaching abroad primarily adopted a transmission model, transmitting geographical knowledge and skills. These examples raise two important issues for the development of intercultural citizenship through language teaching. Firstly, time spent teaching abroad has the potential to positively impact on the development of teachers' skills and perhaps also their conviction of the importance of promoting citizenship. Many language teachers will have spent a period of time abroad as part of their subject training. Additional integration of intercultural experiences in language teacher education can provide meaningful opportunities for critical reflection on the teachers' own reactions to such experiences, but also on how such experiences can shape language-for-citizenship pedagogy. The obvious next question that arises is the extent to which teachers are equipped to deliver these pedagogies. Language teaching that focuses on the acquisition of functions and systems can all too readily take a transmissive form, restricting learners' participation to pre-determined, highly structured interactions focused on topics of limited intellectual challenge. Hennebry (2012) found that, while language teachers felt confident to teach about other cultures, they were notably less so with regard to developing skills for active citizenship. Walkington and Wilkins (2000) suggest that teacher education interventions play an important part in effective citizenship education, equipping teachers with strategies for participatory teaching styles. Language teacher education currently gives little attention to the preparation of teachers for addressing intercultural citizenship matters in the language classroom.

## IMPLICATIONS FOR TEACHERS

Effective pedagogy begins with teachers' professional beliefs and convictions. The enactment of language teaching for citizenship will depend on the extent to which teachers believe they are capable of the task and have, moreover, understood that they have a part to play in shaping their students for whole citizenship, rather than preparing them to be merely language learners. Language learning for intercultural citizenship requires 'an understanding of culture as facts, artifacts, information and social practices, as well as an understanding of culture as the lens through which people mutually interpret and communicate meaning' (Liddicoat and Scarino 2013: 46). Teachers need to see language teaching as more than the teaching of linguistic systems, but rather as the means within their expertise that would allow them to sow the seeds for forging constructive intercultural dialogue and collaboration through which individuals and society thrive.

Teachers play a key role in learners' psychosocial development, not least through modelling relationships through classroom interactions. Teaching the skills and attitudes for intercultural citizenship demands that teachers first possess them themselves. The first point of consideration in preparing for intercultural citizenship is teachers' own competence in intercultural matters. Elena (2014) observes that while individuals in a class may at times share the same language and perhaps even a similar national culture, each individual nevertheless brings and communicates their own individual culture in terms of family, social backgrounds, learning experiences, and so on. As such, teachers are and have always been involved in the process of negotiating intercultural perspectives and relationships with the goal of promoting and maintaining social harmony; they have in this sense always been 'intercultural' and are already equipped with the first crucial attribute. This is particularly true of language teachers, who in many cases have also had extended, first-hand intercultural experiences as part of their subject training.

In the collaboration between intercultural citizenship and language teaching, teachers are required to develop an informed awareness of their teaching practices, aims and identities (Elena 2014) and to extend their own intercultural skills to their students.

Much language teaching is dominated by attention to linguistic systems, driven in part by teachers' own experiences of a declarative pedagogy for language learning and by the washback effect of examinations and tests. Language teachers must also be aware of all the dimensions of the language-culture nexus (Risager 2006, 2007; Kramsch 2011). As Byram and Wagner (2018) point out, learners typically acquire one version of a language as used in one context, usually by the 'native' speaker in the 'national' context, towards which learners are expected to adjust their language use.

Discussions around the notion of linguae francae have challenged this limited view of linguistic communities. While it remains unclear how the ideas generated through such discussions can clearly and specifically translate to pedagogy, they nevertheless offer an entry point raising students' awareness of the interaction between identity, culture and language and the ways in which language use can communicate meanings and bring about diverse effects in terms of building intercultural relationships. While transiting along this process, it is also very important that teachers do not forget and give due consideration to students' own identities. Language learning should never be a process whereby students are required to leave their own identities at the door, but instead teachers need to carefully and respectfully consider how their existing languages shape students' identities and the role that language education plays in fostering assured personal growth or in negatively denying these identities. Teachers and learners need to engage in a process of negotiating existing and new languages and identities.

Many language teachers already understand the potential that is inherent to language learning for building intercultural citizenship education but may find it challenging to integrate this dimension into their teaching, perhaps due to a lack of experience, expertise or professional self-efficacy in this particular area due to curriculum constraints, a heavy focus on exam performance or even due to an absence of collaborative structures.

Seeking out professional development opportunities where school support is available can be helpful in allowing teachers the time and space to step back and reflect on what such a shift would entail for pedagogy and for classroom priorities. Time and thinking space for promoting reflective practice that leads to effective teaching are two rare but crucial commodities in today's educational institutions. Language departments would do well to collaboratively re-examine their learning objectives, syllabuses and materials, in order to critically examine the extent to which the existing content and design aligns with the needs of their students as they leave the classroom. Collaboration with teachers in other curriculum areas such as citizenship, history, geography and others, can also offer structures within which to foster inspiration and creativity for an integrative and cohesive approach, allowing students to experience the existence and application of knowledge and to see the interrelatedness of learning. Teachers across languages can also foster productive collaboration that points to the complementary nature of teaching skills and attitudes in intercultural competence even across parts of different areas of knowledge components. Language teachers need to provide students with opportunities to develop their language skills and their identity through interactions with those of other cultural affiliations. In so doing, students come to value language learning as a means of developing and communicating their identity, rather than as a code designed for use only in restricted environments.

Today's language teachers need to rethink and continue to research and develop their own professional identities in a continuous process of enhancement, reaching new and interesting points along their professional pathways. Simply teaching a language and its discrete aspects for possible use at a later stage is no longer enough. Instead, language teachers need to be able to respond to the educational, social and developmental significance of language teaching in today's global context, helping students to reflect critically on their own identity and on the dynamic processes of communication in which they engage, making language teaching directly relevant to their learners' worlds. Learners need to see language learning as an important part of their education and something they can use right now and continually into the future as an integrated part of their identities. Language teachers will perhaps need to step out of their comfort zone, exploring unfamiliar content with students or collaborating with colleagues in unfamiliar curriculum areas. In this endeavour the intercultural skills teachers already apply in negotiating their culturally diverse classrooms will provide a useful resource.

## IMPLICATIONS FOR CURRICULUM DESIGN

Over thirty years ago, van Ek (1986) pointed to the gap between the 'lofty ideals' of prefaces to curricula and the way these translate, or not, into the workings of the curriculum to later spill, or not, into the language classroom. Research evidence has suggested that this situation remains the case today (Hennebry 2011, 2014). Curricula introductions reference intercultural understanding, while the focus throughout the rest of the document remains squarely on language competence (Byram and Wagner 2018).

The nature of language curricula would benefit from re-examination. It is undoubtedly important to equip learners with linguistic competence for effective intercultural communication. Nevertheless, this needs to be balanced against the need to outline a curriculum at an appropriate level of cognitive demand due to the learners to whom it is addressed. Starkey (2002) expresses his concern that language curriculum topics too often infantilise learners, requiring them to engage with topics considerably below their cognitive capacities. He outlines the 'trimming' of the National Curriculum for Modern Foreign Languages in England which reduced the potentially interesting and ambitious topics such as 'international world', 'communications' and 'imagination and creativity' down to the language of the classroom, home life and school, food, health and fitness, and so on. While these topics could themselves be developed into challenging and engaging areas of exploration, the trimming that took place in 1995, with the first revision of the National Curriculum, has yet to see the intellectual value of language learning reinstated. Careful work needs to be done in order to align an intellectually engaging curriculum content with students' expected level of linguistic proficiency. In contexts where language lessons are given very little room on the school timetable, the reality is that students may not achieve levels of proficiency adequate for effective communication, thus making failure an inevitable consequence if the goal is to promote communicative competence. On the other hand, if the goal is to provide students with an entry point for effective intercultural understanding, then some of the existing curricula may also be setting learners up for inevitable failure. Curriculum design and development require careful reflection on the learning outcomes that are meaningful and feasible given the challenges and opportunities of real classroom contexts.

Models such as content-based instruction (e.g. Snow 2001) or Content and Language Integrated Learning (CLIL) (e.g. Coyle 2007) provide the means through which cognitively and emotionally demanding content can be introduced into the language classroom. Through these models, language learners can engage with issues such as the environment (Porto et al. 2017) or historical and socio-economic conflicts (Porto and Yulita 2017) in their own country and in relation to other countries, enabling them to develop linguistic proficiency, as well as the knowledge, skills and attitudes of an intercultural speaker. Rauschert and Byram (2018) propose that through this process students can be encouraged to engage directly with their own and other communities, responding to what they have learned in action by experience and practice from their immediate community.

Byram and Wagner (2018) point out the important parallels between developing intercultural citizenship and the fostering of social values – such as those mentioned before – as common, desirable aims for many schools in diverse settings, when addressing the citizenship curriculum. This takes place across a range of curriculum areas. They argue that educators working towards each of these concepts support students in reflecting critically on language, discourse and culture with regard to power and inequality. The relationship between language education and education for citizenship and between intercultural citizenship and the development of critical thinking on the subject is well established (Byram et al. 2017) and offers a context for cross-curricular collaboration. Cross-curricular teaching offers opportunities for teachers to support one another's professional development. Language teachers have linguistic expertise and direct experience of other cultures and worldviews that can transport language learners beyond their immediate confines. Citizenship teachers, on the other hand, are trained in participatory pedagogies for effective citizenship education, such as the pedagogy of process that prioritises the creation of supportive environments conducive to active and inclusive participation (Kalantzis and Cope 1999; Nieto 2010).

Approaches such as Intercultural Service Learning and intercultural citizenship education have been found to be effective in fostering foreign-language education, intercultural learning and citizenship competences (e.g. Porto 2014; Rauschert 2014; Porto and Byram 2015). Nevertheless, integrating such approaches into curriculum design presents a range of practical challenges relating to teacher expertise, logistical challenges, curriculum design and methodology. Teachers working within these approaches operate as advisors and mentors, demanding a reconceptualisation of their professional identity (Bohl and Kucharz 2010) and requiring teacher education to integrate the necessary skills to such aims. These approaches also necessitate establishing international relations that can in turn facilitate the development of projects with mid- to long-term objectives, enabling substantial learning experiences, both of which are significant demands.

The skills, time and focus that Service Learning projects demand would need considerable re-examination (Seifert and Zentner 2010: 33). Here again a content-based approach could well provide the necessary structures and pedagogies for promoting experiential citizenship education through language teaching, helping students to develop language skills but also to become active intercultural citizens, engaged in society (Byram 2009: 130).

## IMPLICATIONS FOR RESEARCH AND THEORY

While there exist models for understanding intercultural citizenship, a more precise definition that accounts also for the role of learning is needed, particularly one that explicitly outlines the learning theories that underpin it, and the ways in which the model might be applied in classroom contexts (Wagner, Conlon Perugini and Byram 2017). Existing models of intercultural competence, particularly Byram's (1997) model, have been helpful for the purposes of planning a cultural dimension into language teaching methods (Spitzberg and Changnon 2009) and in pointing to the crucial aspect of critical reflection on the learners' own and on others' perspectives. Yet, further work will be required, firstly to make explicit the learning theories that underpin these models and secondly to integrate intercultural competence into a broader model of active intercultural citizenship. Byram and Wagner (2018) suggest bringing an action-oriented approach underpinned by citizenship education and framed by theories of experiential learning, and to apply these to the teaching of intercultural citizenship. Further theorisation as well as systematic, intervention research would provide a more robust evidence base for developing a more effective pedagogy and curriculum planning.

## IMPLICATIONS FOR POLICY MAKERS

Policy across diverse cultural contexts highlights the need for language teaching to play a central role in quipping students with the skills and knowledge for active participation in today's society locally, nationally, supra-nationally and globally. In order for those policy statements to become a meaningful reality in classrooms and in the lives of teachers and students, resources need to be made available to enable systematic and continuous professional development specifically targeted at this concern. The time allocated to language teaching in the school curriculum would probably need to be increased in order to enable teachers feasibly to do the work of identity formation and negotiation with their students, as well as to encourage the development of the critical thinking skills that lie at the heart of intercultural citizenship.

Funding also may require a proportional increase commensurate to the possibilities available to support international collaborations that enable sustained exposure to and interaction with other cultural contexts. Standardised national assessments need to reflect the importance of language learning and of the acquisition of the tools for intercultural citizenship in a form and content that would support individuals and groups accordingly to thrive and prosper with such advantageous skills in the global arena.

In short, policy makers need to ensure that the necessary conditions on the ground are in place and that these efforts will be sustainable so that policies can be feasibly enacted. Statements of lofty goals that are not rooted in real and practical support for teachers risk alienating teachers and learners from the mission of education as they struggle to negotiate between the ideal and the reality. Effective integration of language teaching and intercultural citizenship education will only become a meaningful reality if teachers, learners, policy makers and teacher educators work together to make it possible. No greater motivation for this should be necessary than the urgent global demand for citizens who can play their part in forging a peaceful, harmonious society marked by clear values that work to the common good and a humility that enables respect and appreciation for others.

## CONCLUDING THOUGHTS

The relationship between language education and citizenship which is at the core of this book appears to be based on an interest to know more about different communities on the part of the learner, and on a professional aptitude to share knowledge and experience on the diverse ways of living and communicating on the part of the teacher. As these two corresponding attitudes click and fuse together a symbiotic movement takes place, knowledge and experiences are acquired and reinforced, and human beings and groupings become more empowered as they become more understanding and knowledgeable in how to communicate and interact effectively.

The isolating effects of monolingualism are defeated by such attitudes even before the second language is fully acquired; even a native English speaker could find a variety of cultures expressed in that language. The United Kingdom, the United States, Canada, Australia, New Zealand, Ireland and several other fascinating island cultures express themselves in the same language, English, to communicate a variety of very distinct societies where the same language is used to name very different realities. Therefore, we are seeking a disposition, an attitude of the mind. This inclination of the mind appears to be a condition for the learning of citizenship also, a reflective perception of the importance of the learner's own culture and of its pre-eminent place that can be fully realised only within the rich variety of other culture's recognition.

These other cultures exist wherever human groupings have established a modality of community life, and learners need to be prepared to discover them within, on and beyond arbitrary frontiers. As such, different languages spoken within the same country, diverse dialects and other foreign languages contribute to the knowledge and richness of cultures that basically are expressions evidencing the outputs of 'others-like-me' throughout different historical communities.

*When the school introduces and trains each child of society into membership within such a little community, saturating him with the spirit of service, and providing him with the instrument of effective self-direction, we shall have the deepest and best guarantee of a larger society which is worthy, lovely, and harmonious.*
(Dewey 1907: 44)

# Bibliography


Advisory Group on the Teaching of Citizenship and Democracy in Schools (1998). *The Advisory Group for Citizenship Report (Crick Report).* London: Qualifications and Curriculum Authority. Downloaded at: https://www.teachingcitizenship.org.uk/sites/teachingcitizenship.org.uk/files/6123_crick_report_1998_0.pdf

Agar, M. (1996). *The Professional Stranger: An Informal Introduction to Ethnography.* New York: Academic Press.

Ajegbo, K., Kiwan, D. and Sharma, S. (2007) *Diversity and Citizenship Curriculum Review.* Nottingham: Department for Education and Skills. Downloaded at: http://www.educationengland.org.uk/documents/pdfs/2007-ajegbo-report-citizenship.pdf

Aktas, F., Pitts, K., Richards, J. C. and Silova, I. (2017). Institutionalizing global citizenship: A critical analysis of higher education programs and curricula. *Journal of Studies in International Education, 21*(1), 65–80.

Andreotti, V. (2006). Soft versus critical global citizenship education. *Policy & Practice: A Development Education Review, 3*, 40–51.

Appadurai, A. (2000). Grassroots globalization and the research imagination. *Public Culture, 12*(1), 1–19.

Appiah, A. (2006). *Cosmopolitanism: Ethics in a World of Strangers.* London: Penguin.

Árva, V. and Medgyes, P. (2000). Native and non-native teachers in the classroom. *System, 28*(3), 355–372.

Atay, D. (2007). Beginning teacher efficacy and the practicum in an EFL context. *Teacher Development, 11*(2), 203–219.

Austin, A. (2012). Challenges and visions for higher education in a complex world: Commentary on Barnett and Barrie. *Higher Education Research & Development, 31*, 57–67.

Baker, C. (2011). *Foundations of Bilingual Education and Bilingualism* (5th ed.). Clevedon, UK: Multilingual Matters.

Bandura, A. (2001). *Guide for Constructing Self-efficacy Scales.* Stanford, CA: Stanford University.

Barber, B. (1984). *Strong Democracy: Participatory Politics for a New Age.* Los Angeles: University of California Press.

Behrnd, V. and Porzelt, S. (2012). Intercultural competence and training outcomes of students with experiences abroad. *International Journal of Intercultural Relations, 36*(2), 213–223.

Bellamy, R. (2008). Evaluating union citizenship: Belonging, rights and participation within the EU. *Citizenship Studies, 12*(6), 597–611.

Billig, S. H. (2010). Why service learning is such a good idea. *Grand Valley State University Colleagues Magazine, 5* (summer/fall), 9–11.

Blackledge, A. (2004). Constructions of identity in political discourse in multilingual Britain.

In A. Pavlenko and A. Blackledge (eds), *Negotiation of Identities in Multilingual Contexts* (pp. 68–92). Clevedon, UK: Multilingual Matters.

Blommaert, J. and Verschueren, J. (1998). *Debating Diversity*. London: Routledge.

Blunkett, D. and Taylor, M. (2010). Active citizenship and Labour. Active Citizenship: What Could It Achieve and How, 26–38.

Bohl, T. and Kucharz, D. (2010). *Offener Unterricht heute: konzeptionelle und didaktische Weiterentwicklung*. Beltz Pädagogik: Weinheim.

Boni, A. and Calabuig, C. (2017). Education for global citizenship at universities: Potentialities of formal and informal learning spaces to foster cosmopolitanism. *Journal of Studies in International Education, 21*(1), 22–38.

Bonvillain, N. (2003) *Language, Culture, and Communication: The Meaning of Messages* (4th ed.). Upper Saddle River, NJ: Prentice Hall.

Borg, S. (2003). Teacher cognition in language teaching: A review of research on what language teachers think, know, believe, and do. *Language Teaching, 36*(2), 81–109.

Borg, S. (2006). *Teacher Cognition and Language Education*. London: Continuum.

Bowden, B. (2003). The perils of global citizenship. *Citizenship Studies, 7*, 349–362.

Brandon, W. C. and Clayton, P. H. (2011). Research on and through reflection in International Service Learning. In R. Bringle, J. Hatcher and S. G. Jones (eds), *International Service Learning. Conceptual Frameworks and Research* (pp. 145–187). Sterling, VA: Stylus Publishing.

Breidbach, S. (2002). European communicative integration: The function of foreign language teaching for the development of a European public sphere. *Language, Culture and Curriculum, 15*(3), 273–283.

Brettell, C. (2011). Experiencing everyday discrimination: A comparison across five immigrant populations. *Race and Social Problems, 3*(4), 266–279.

Bringle, R. G. and Hatcher, J. A. (1995). A service-learning curriculum for faculty. *Michigan Journal of Community Service Learning, 2*(1), 112–122.

Brookfield, S. (1988). *Developing Critical Thinkers: Challenging Adults to Explore Alternative Ways of Thinking and Action*. Buckingham: Open University Press.

Brookfield, S. (1995). *Becoming a Critically Reflective Teacher*. San Francisco, CA: Jossey-Bass.

Brubaker, R. and Cooper, F. (2000). Beyond identity. *Theory and Society*, 29(1), 1–47.

Byram, M. (1992). Foreign language learning for European citizenship. *The Language Learning Journal, 6*, 10–12.

Byram, M. (1997). *Teaching and Assessing Intercultural Communicative Competence*. Clevedon, UK: Multilingual Matters.

Byram, M. (1998). *Cultural Studies in Foreign Language Education*. Clevedon, UK: Multilingual Matters.

Byram, M. (2000). Assessing intercultural competence in language teaching. *Sprogforum, 18*(6), 8–13.

Byram, M. (2001). Language teaching as a political action. In M. Bax and J. Zwart (eds), *Reflections on Language and Language Learning. In Honour of Arthur van Essen* (pp. 91–104). Amsterdam/Philadelphia, PA: John Benjamins.

Byram, M. (2008). *From Foreign Language Education to Education for Intercultural Citizenship. Essays and Reflections*. Clevedon, UK: Multilingual Matters.

Byram, M. (2009). Intercultural competence in foreign languages. The intercultural speaker and the pedagogy of foreign language education. In D. Deardorff (ed.), *The SAGE Handbook of Intercultural Competence* (pp. 321–332). Thousand Oaks, CA: SAGE.

Byram, M. (2014). Competence, interaction and action: Developing intercultural citizenship education in the language classroom and beyond. In X. Dai and G. Chen (eds), *Intercultural Communication Competence: Conceptualization and its Development in Cultural Contexts and Interactions* (pp. 190–198). Newcastle-upon-Tyne, UK: Cambridge Scholars Publishing.

Byram, M. and Wagner, M. (2018). Making a difference: Language teaching for intercultural and international dialogue. *Foreign Language Annals*, *51*, 140–151.

Byram, M., Gribkova, B. and Starkey, H. (2002). Developing the Intercultural Dimension in Language Teaching – A Practical Introduction for Teachers. Language Policy Division, Directorate of School, Out-of-School and Higher Education, DGIV, Council of Europe, Strasbourg.

Byram, M., Golubeva, I. Han, H. and Wagner, M. (eds) (2017). *From Principles to Practice in Education for Intercultural Citizenship*. Clevedon, UK: Multilingual Matters.

Byrne, B. (2014). *Making Citizens: Public Rituals and Personal Journeys to Citizenship*. Basingstoke: Palgrave Macmillan.

Calhoun, C. (2003). 'Belonging' in the cosmopolitan imaginary. *Ethnicities*, *3*, 531–568.

Canagarajah, S. (2011). Codemeshing in academic writing: Identifying teachable strategies of translanguaging. *The Modern Language Journal*, *95*(3), 401–417.

Candelier, M. (2008). Approches plurielles, didactique du plurilinguisme. *Les Cahiers de l'Acedle*, *5*(1), 65–90.

Care, A. (2017). 'Brits should learn Polish or Urdu to help encourage integration', says Cambridge linguistics professor. Downloaded at: https://www.cambridge-news.co.uk/news/cambridge-news/brits-should-learn-polish-urdu-12464508

Castles, S. (2004). Migration, citizenship, and education. In J. A. Banks (ed.), *Diversity and Citizenship Education: Global Perspectives* (pp. 17–48). San Francisco, CA: Jossey-Bass.

Chacon, C. (2005). Teachers' perceived efficacy among English as foreign language teachers in middle schools in Venezuela. *Teaching and Teacher Education*, *21*, 257–272.

Chen, J. F., Warden, C. A. and Chang, H.-T. (2005). Motivators that do not motivate: The case of Chinese EFL learners and the influence of culture on motivation. *TESOL Quarterly*, *39*(4), 609–633.

Cheong, P. H., Edwards, R., Goulbourne, H. and Solomos, J. (2007). Immigration, social cohesion and social capital: A critical review. *Critical Social Policy*, *27*(1), 24–49.

Chesterton, G. K. (1909). *The Collected Works Vol. 28*. San Francisco, CA: Ignatius Press.

Coleman, J. A., Galaczi, Á. and Astruc, L. (2007). Motivation of UK school pupils towards foreign languages: A large-scale survey at Key Stage 3. *Language Learning Journal*, *35*(2), 245–281.

Commission of the European Communities (1993). Green Paper on the European Dimension of Education. Brussels.

Commission of the European Communities (2008). *Progress Towards the Lisbon Objectives in Education and Training: Indicators and Benchmarks*. Brussels.

Convery, A., Evans, M., Green, S., Macaro, E. and Mellor, J. (1997). *Pupils' Perceptions of Europe: Identity and Education*. London: Cassell Education.

Convey, A. and Merritt, A. (2000). The United Kingdom. In C. Brock and W. Tulasiewicz (eds), *Education in a Single Europe* (2nd ed.). London: Routledge.

Coryell, J. E., Spencer, B. J. and Sehin, O. (2014). Cosmopolitan adult education and global citizenship: Perceptions from a European itinerant graduate professional study abroad program. *Adult Education Quarterly*, *64*(2), 145–164.

Council of the European Union (2004). Education & Training 2010: Joint Interim Report of the Council and the Commission on the implementation of the Detailed Work Programme on the Follow-up of the Objectives of Education and Training Systems in Europe. Brussels.

Council of Europe (2009). Autobiography of Intercultural Encounters. Downloaded at: http://www.coe.int/dialogue

Coyle, D. (2007). Content and language integrated learning: Towards a connected research agenda for CLIL pedagogies. *International Journal of Bilingual Education and Bilingualism*, *10*(5), 543–562.

Coyle, D., Holmes, B. and King, L. (2009). Towards an Integrated Curriculum – CLIL

National Statement and Guidelines. Downloaded at: https://www.unifg.it/sites/default/files/allegatiparagrafo/20-01-2014/coyle_et_al_towards_an_integrated_curriculum_clil_national_statement_and_guidelines.pdf

Crandall, J. (1994). Strategic integration: Preparing language and content teachers for linguistically and culturally diverse classrooms. In J. E. Alatis (ed.), *Strategic Interaction and Language Acquisition: Theory, Practice, and Research* (pp. 255–274). Washington, DC: Georgetown University Press.

Crandall, J. (2000). Language teacher education. *Annual Review of Applied Linguistics, 20*, 34–55.

Creanza, M. A. (1997). La motivazione all'apprendimento della lingua inglese nella scuola superiore. *Rassegna Italiana di Linguistica Applicata, 29*(3), 97–114.

Creese, A. and Blackledge, A. (2015). Translanguaging and identity in educational settings. *Annual Review of Applied Linguistics, 35*, 20–35.

Crewe, I., Searing, D. and Conover, P. (1997). Colloquium on Education and Citizenship: Citizenship and Civic Education. *Citizenship Education.* London: The Citizenship Foundation.

Crick, B. (2000). *Essays on Citizenship.* London: Continuum.

Crick, B. and Lockyer, A. (2010). *Active Citizenship: What Could it Achieve and How?* Edinburgh: Edinburgh University Press.

Crozet, C. and Liddicoat, A. J. (2000). Teaching culture as an integrated part of language: Implications for the aims, approaches and pedagogies of language teaching. In A. J. Liddicoat and C. Crozet (eds), *Teaching Languages, Teaching Cultures* (pp. 1–18). Melbourne, Victoria: Applied Linguistics Association of Australia.

Crystal, D. (1997). *English as a Global Language.* Cambridge: Cambridge University Press.

Curriculum Development Council (2002). *Basic Education Curriculum Guide.* Hong Kong: Education Bureau.

Curriculum Development Council (2017). *English Language Education: Key Learning Area Curriculum Guide (Primary 1–Secondary 6).* Downloaded at: https://www.edb.gov.hk/attachment/en/curriculum-development/renewal/ELE/ELE_KLACG_P1-S6_Eng_2017.pdf.

Curriculum Development Council and the Hong Kong Examinations and Assessment Authority (2007). *English Language Curriculum and Assessment Guide (Secondary 4–6).* Downloaded at: http://www.hkeaa.edu.hk/DocLibrary/SBA/HKDSE/Eng_DVD/doc/HKEAA_eng_lang_final.pdf

Darvin, R. and Norton, B. (2016). Identity, language learning, and critical pedagogies in digital times. In J. Cenoz, G. Gorter and S. May (eds), *Language Awareness and Multilingualism* (pp. 1–12). Switzerland: Springer International Publishing.

Davies, A. (2003). *The Native Speaker: Myth and Reality* (Vol. 38). Clevedon, UK: Multilingual Matters.

Deardorff, D., de Wit, H. and Heyl, J. (2012). Bridges to the future: The global landscape of international higher education. In D. Deardorff, H. de Wit, J. Heyl and T. Adams (eds), *The SAGE Handbook of International Higher Education* (pp. 457–485). Thousand Oaks, CA: Sage.

De Britos, A. (2016). Mother Tongue Other Tongue multilingual project for schools: Add your voice to the Poet-Tree. *Scottish Languages Review, 31*, 43–52.

Delors, J. (1996). *Learning: The Treasure Within.* Paris: UNESCO.

Department for Education (2013). *Modern Foreign Language Programmes of Study.* Downloaded at: http://www.education.gov.uk/schools/teachingandlearning/curriculum/secondary/b00199616/mfl/programme (accessed 1 September 2016).

Department for Education (2014). Promoting fundamental British values as part of SMSC in schools, ref. DFE-00679-2014. Downloaded at: https://www.gov.uk/government/publications/promoting-fundamental-british-values-through-smsc

Department for Education and Skills (1997). White Paper: Excellence in Schools. Downloaded at: http://www.educationengland.org.uk/documents/wp1997/excellence-in-schools.html

Dewey, J. (1907). *The School and Society*. Chicago: Chicago Press.

Dewey, J. (1916). *Democracy and Education: An Introduction to the Philosophy of Education*. New York: Macmillan.

Dewey, J. (1938). *Experience and Education*. New York: Kappa Delta Pi.

De Wit, H., Hunter, F., Jones, E. and Leask, B. (2013). Advancing Global Citizenship through Internationalisation in Higher Education: Definitions, Models, Challenges and Practices: A Literature Review. (Unpublished report.) Report prepared by the Centre for Higher Education Internationalisation for the International Network of Universities.

Dörnyei, Z. (2009). The L2 Motivational Self System. In Z. Dörnyei and E. Ushioda (eds), *Motivation, Language Identity and the L2 Self* (pp. 9–42). Clevedon, UK: Multilingual Matters.

Dörnyei, Z. and Ryan, S. (2015). *The Psychology of the Language Learner Revisited*. New York: Routledge.

Dörnyei, Z. and Ushioda, E. (2011). *Teaching and Researching Motivation* (2nd ed.). Harlow, UK: Longman.

Dwyer, P. (2000). *Welfare Rights and Responsibilities: Contesting Social Citizenship*. Bristol: The Policy Press.

Dwyer, P. (2010). *Understanding Social Citizenship* (2nd ed.). Bristol: The Policy Press.

Education Bureau (2001). *Learning to Learn: The Way Forward in Curriculum Development*. Downloaded at: https://cd1.edb.hkedcity.net/cd/EN/Content_2908/e00/chairman.pdf

Elena, S. (2014). The 'intercultural' teacher – A new response to the teaching career. *Procedia-Social and Behavioral Sciences*, *128*, 111–116.

Eriksen, T. H. (2006) Diversity versus difference: Neo-liberalism in the minority debate. In R. Rottenburg, E. Schnepel and S. Shimada (eds), *The Making and Unmaking of Difference* (pp. 13–36). Bielefeld: Transcript.

Eslami, Z. and Fatahi, A. (2008). Teachers' sense of self-efficacy, English proficiency, and instructional strategies: A study of nonnative EFL teachers in Iran. *TESL-EJ*, *11*(4), 1–19.

European Commission (1995). The 1995 White Paper on Education. Brussels: The European Commission.

European Commission (2016). *Europe for Citizens Programme*. Downloaded at: http://ec.europa.eu/citizenship/europe-for-citizens-programme/ (accessed 30 September 2017).

Evans, M., Schneider, C., Arnot, M., Fisher, L., Forbes, K., Hu, M. and Liu, Y. (2016). *Language Development and School Achievement: Opportunities and Challenges in the Education of EAL Students*. Cambridge: The Bell Foundation.

Faez, F. and Valeo, A. (2012). TESOL teacher education: Novice teachers' perceptions of their preparedness and efficacy in the classroom. *TESOL Quarterly*, *46*(3), 450–471.

Fairbrother, G. P. (2014). The Chinese paternalistic state and moral education. In K. J. Kennedy, G. P. Fairbrother and Z. Zhenxhou (eds), *Citizenship Education in China: Preparing Citizens for the 'Chinese Century'* (pp. 11–27). Abingdon: Routledge.

Fairclough, N. (1995) *Critical Discourse Analysis: The Critical Study of Language*. London/New York: Longman.

Fantini, A. (2000). A central concern: Developing intercultural competence. *SIT Occasional Papers Series*, 1 (spring), 25–42.

Faulks, K. (2000). *Citizenship*. New York: Routledge.

Finnish National Board of Education (2004). *National Core Curriculum for Basic Education*. Downloaded at: http://www.oph.fi/download/47672_core_curricula_basic_education_3.pdf (accessed 1 September 2016).

Feryok, A. (2010). Language teacher cognitions: Complex dynamic systems? *System*, *38*(2), 272–279.

Fishman, J. A., Cooper, R. L. and Conrad, A. W. (1977). *The Spread of English: The Sociology of English as an Additional Language*. Rowley, M: Newbury House Publishers.
Flores, M. and Day, C. (2006). Contexts which shape and reshape new teachers' identities: A multi-perspective study. *Teaching and Teacher Education, 22*(2), 219–232.
Foucault, M. (1980). *Power/Knowledge: Selected Interviews and Other Writings, 1972–1977*. New York: Pantheon Books.
Freedman, S. and Appleman, D. (2008). 'What else will I be doing?': Teacher identity and teacher retention in urban schools. *Teacher Education Quarterly, 35*(3), 109–126.
Freeman, D. (1998). *Doing Teacher Research: From Inquiry to Understanding*. Boston, MA: Heinle and Heinle.
Furco, A. (2003). Issues of definition and program diversity in the study of Service-Learning. In S. Billig and A. S. Waterman (eds), *Studying Service-learning: Innovations in Education Research Methodology* (pp. 11–30). Mahwah, NJ: Lawrence Erlbaum Associates.
Gacel-Ávila, J. (2005). The internationalisation of higher education: A paradigm for global citizenry. *Journal of Studies in International Education, 9*(2), 121–136.
Galloway, N. and Rose, H. (2015). *Introducing Global Englishes*. London: Routledge.
García, O. (1997). Bilingual education. In F. Coulmas (ed.), *The Handbook of Sociolinguistics* (pp. 405–420). Oxford: Blackwell Publishers Ltd.
García, O. (2009). Education, multilingualism and translanguaging in the 21st century. In T. Skutnab-Kangas, R. Phillipson, A. K. Mohanty and M. Panda (eds), *Social Justice through Multilingual Education*. Clevedon, UK: Multilingual Matters.
García, O. and Sylvan, C. (2011). Pedagogies and practices in multilingual classrooms: Singularities and pluralities. *The Modern Language Journal, 95*(3), 385–400.
Gardner, R. C. (1985). *Social Psychology and Second Language Learning: The Role of Attitudes and Motivation*. London: Edward Arnold.
Gardner, R. C. (2010). *Motivation and Second Language Acquisition: The Socio-educational Model*. New York: Peter Lang Publishing.
Gardner, R. C. and MacIntyre, P. D. (1993). A student's contribution to second language learning. Part II: Affective variables. *Language Teaching, 26*, 1–11.
Gee, J. P. (2005). *An Introduction to Discourse Analysis: Theory and Method* (2nd ed). New York: Routledge/Taylor and Francis Group.
Gibbs, G. (1988). *Learning by Doing: A Guide to Teaching and Learning Methods*. Downloaded at: http://www2.glos.ac.uk/gdn/gibbs/ch4_3.htm
Gilbertson, G. and Singer, A. (2003). The emergence of protective citizenship in the USA: Naturalization among Dominican immigrants in the post-1996 welfare reform era. *Ethnic and Racial Studies, 26*(1), 25–51.
Golombek, P. and Doran, M. (2014). Unifying cognition, emotion, and activity in language teacher professional development. *Teaching and Teacher Education, 39*, 102–111.
Gonzalez, N., Moll, L. and Amanti, C. (2005). *Funds of Knowledge*. Mahwah, NJ: Erlbaum.
Gorman, R. F. (1992). Citizenship, obligation and exile in the Greek and Roman experience. *Public Affairs Quarterly, 6*(1), 5–22.
Gray, D. and Griffin, C. (2014). A journey to citizenship: Constructions of citizenship and identity in the British citizenship test. *British Journal of Social Psychology, 53*(2), 299–314.
Great British Home Office (2013). *Life in the United Kingdom. A Guide for New Residents*. London: UK Government.
Griffin, J. (2016). Hold your tongues: Why language learners fear a vote for Brexit. Downloaded at :https://www.theguardian.com/media/mind-your-language/2016/jun/21/hold-your-tongues-why-language-learners-fear-a-vote-for-brexit
Guerrero, C. H. (2010). Elite vs. folk bilingualism: The mismatch between theories and educational and social conditions. *How Journal, 17*(1), 165–179.
Guilherme, M. (2002). *Critical Citizens for an Intercultural World: Foreign Language Education as Cultural Politics*. Clevedon, UK: Multilingual Matters.

Haigh, M. (2014). From internationalisation to education for global citizenship: A multi-layered history. *Higher Education Quarterly, 68*(1), 6–27.

Hall, S., Evans, J. and Nixon, S. (eds) (2013). *Representation: Cultural Representations and Signifying Practices* (5th ed.). Los Angeles, CA: Sage.

Hammerness, K., Darling-Hammond, L., Bransford, J., Berliner, D., Cochran-Smith, M., McDonald, M. and Kenneth, Z. (2005). How teachers learn and develop. In L. Darling-Hammond and J. Bransford (eds), *Preparing Teachers for a Changing World: What Teachers Should Learn and be Able to Do* (pp. 258–289). San Francisco, CA: Jossey-Bass.

Heater, D. (1990). *Citizenship: the Civic Ideal in World History, Politics and Education.* Harlow, UK: Longman.

Heater, D. (1992). Education for European citizenship. *Westminster Studies in Education, 15*, 53–67.

Heater, D. (1999). *What is Citizenship?* Cambridge: Cambridge University Press.

Henderson, J. (2013). Teaching Global Citizenship: A Case Study in Applied Linguistics. Higher Education Academy. Downloaded at: https://www.heacademy.ac.uk/system/files/Global_citizenship_Henderson_.pdf

Hennebry, M. (2011). Interactions between European citizenship and language learning among adolescent Europeans. *European Educational Research Journal, 10*(4), 623–641.

Hennebry, M. (2012). The perspectives of practitioners on the teaching of European citizenship through Modern Foreign Languages. In J. Sayer and L. Erler (eds), *Schools for the Future Europe* (pp. 100–116). London: Continuum.

Hennebry, M. (2013). Cultural awareness – should it be taught? Can it be taught? In E. Macaro, P. Driscoll and A. Swarbrick (eds), *Language Learning: Research, Policy and Practice* (pp. 135–149). London: Routledge.

Hennebry, M. (2014). Language teaching for European citizenship: Insights for teacher education. *Language Learning Journal, 42*(3), 289–306.

Herbst, K. C., Gaertner, L. and Insko, C. A. (2003). My head says yes but my heart says no: Cognitive and affective attraction as a function of similarity to the ideal self. *Journal of Personality and Social Psychology, 84*, 1206–1219.

Higgins, E. T., Roney, C., Crowe, E. and Hymes, C. (1994). Ideal versus ought predilections for approach and avoidance: Distinct self-regulatory systems. *Journal of Personality and Social Psychology, 66*, 276–286.

Holliday, A. (2006). Native-speakerism. *ELT Journal, 60*(4), 385–387.

Holmes, P. (2014). Intercultural dialogue: Challenges to theory, practice and research. *Language and intercultural communication, 14*(1), 1–6.

Hong Kong Government (2016). Hong Kong the Facts. Downloaded at: https://www.gov.hk/en/about/abouthk/facts.htm (accessed 11 September 2017).

Horner, K. (2015). Discourses on language and citizenship in Europe. *Language and Linguistics Compass, 9*(5), 209–218.

House of Commons Education and Skills Committee (2007). *Citizenship Education: Second Report of Session 2006–2007.* London: The Stationary Office.

House of Lords European Union Select Committee (2005, 14 April). Proposed EU Integrated Action Programme for Life-long Learning. London. Downloaded at: http://www.publications.parliament.uk/ pa/ld200405/ldselect/ldeucom/104/104i.pdf

Huber-Kriegler, M., Lázár, I. and Strange, J. (2003). *Mirrors and Windows: An Intercultural Communication Textbook.* Strasbourg: Council of Europe.

Hufiesen, B. (2011). Gesamtsprachencurriculum: weitere Überlegungen zu einem prototypischen Modell. In R. S. Baur and B. Hufiesen (eds), *'Vieles ist sehr ähnlich.' Individuelle und gesellschaftliche Mehrsprachigkeit als bildungspolitische Aufgabe* (pp. 265–282). Hohengehren: Schneider.

Iannelli, C. and Huang, J. (2014). Trends in participation and attainment of Chinese students in UK higher education. *Studies in Higher Education, 39*(5), 805–822.

Ibrahim, T. (2005). Global citizenship education: Mainstreaming the curriculum? *Cambridge Journal of Education, 35*(2), 177–194.

Ingleby, D. (2000). *Psychologie en de multiculturele samenleving: een gemisteaansluiting?* Utrecht: Ceres.

Ireland, E., Kerr, D., Lopes, J. and Nelson, J., with Cleaver, E. (2006). Active citizenship and young people: Opportunities, experiences and challenges in and beyond school. Citizenship Education Longitudinal Study: Fourth Annual Report. DfES Research Report 732. London: DfES.

Isin, E. F. (2009). Citizenship in flux: The figure of the activist citizen. *Subjectivity, 29*(1), 367–388.

Jacoby, B. and associates (1996). *Service-learning in Higher Education: Concepts and Practices.* San Francisco, CA: Jossey-Bass.

Jamieson, L. (2002). Theorising identity, nationality and citizenship: Implications for European citizenship identity. *Sociología, 34*(6), 507–532.

Janks, H. (1999). Critical discourse analysis as a research tool. In J. Marshall and M. Peters (eds), *Education Policy. The International Library of Comparative Public Policy* (pp. 49–62). Cheltenham, UK: Elgar.

Jansen, T., Chioncel, N. and Dekkers, H. (2006). Social cohesion and integration: Learning active citizenship. *British Journal of Sociology of Education, 27*(02), 189–205.

Jenkins, J., Cogo, A. and Dewey, M. (2011). Review of developments in research into English as a lingua franca. *Language Teaching, 44*(3), 281–315.

Johnson, K. E. (2006). The sociocultural turn and its challenges for second language teacher education. *TESOL Quarterly, 40*(1), 235–257.

Johnson, K. E. and Golombek, P. R. (eds) (2002). *Narrative Inquiry as Professional Development.* New York: Cambridge University Press.

Johnson, K. E. and Golombek, P. R. (eds) (2011). *Research on Second Language Teacher Education.* New York: Routledge.

Jooste, N. and Heleta, S. (2017). Global citizenship versus globally competent graduates: A critical view from the South. *Journal of Studies in International Education, 21*(1), 39–51.

Kachru, B. B. (1986). The power and politics of English. *World Englishes, 5*(2–3), 121–140.

Kahn, H. E. and Agnew, M. (2017). Global learning through difference: Considerations for teaching, learning, and the internationalization of higher education. *Journal of Studies in International Education, 21*(1), 52–64.

Kalantzis, M. and Cope, B. (1999). Multicultural education: Transforming the mainstream. In S. May (ed.), *Critical Multiculturalism: Rethinking Multicultural and Anti-racist Education.* London: Falmer Press.

Kamens, D. H. (1988). Education and democracy: A comparative institutional analysis. *Sociology of Education, 61*(2), 114–127.

Kanno, Y. and Stuart, C. (2011). Learning to become a second language teacher: Identities-in-practice. *The Modern Language Journal, 95*(2), 236–252.

Ke, L. and Starkey, H. (2014). Active citizens, good citizens, and insouciant bystanders: The educational implications of Chinese university students' civic participation via social networking. *London Review of Education, 12*(1), 50-62.

Kelly, M., Grenfell, M., Allen, R., Kriza, C. and McEvoy, W. (2004). European Profile for Language Teacher Education – A Frame of Reference: Final Report. Brussels: European Commission.

Kennedy, K. J., Fairbrother, G. P. and Zhenxhou, Z. (2014). *Citizenship Education in China: Preparing Citizens for the 'Chinese Century'.* Abingdon: Routledge.

Kerr, D. (1999). Changing the political culture: The Advisory Group on Education for Citizenship and the Teaching of Democracy in Schools. *Oxford Review of Education, 25*(1 and 2), 275–284.

Kiely, R., Bechhofer, F., Stewart, R. and McCrone, D. (2001). The markers and rules of Scottish national identity. *The Sociological Review, 49*(1), 33–55.

Klaas, B. and Dirsus, M. (2016). The isolationist catastrophe of 'Brexit'. *Los Angeles Times.* Downloaded at: http://www.latimes.com/opinion/op-ed/la-oe-klaas-dirsus-leave-victory-in-britain-20160623-snap-story.html (accessed 12 March 2018).

Kleppin, K. (2004). Mehrsprachigkeitsdidaktik = Tertiärsprachendidakitik? Zur Verantwortung jeglichen (Fremd-) Sprachenunterrichts für ein Konzept von Mehrsprachigkikeit. Paper presented at the Mehrsprachigkeit im Fokus, Arbeitspapiere der 24. Berlin: Früjahrskonferenz zur Erforschung des Fremdsprachenunterrichts.

Kohn, K. and C. Warth (eds) (2011). *Web Collaboration for Intercultural Language Learning.* Münster, Germany: Monsenstein and Vannerdat.

Kohonen, V. (2000). Towards experiential foreign-language education. In V. Kohonen, R. Jaatinen, P. Kaikkonen and J. Lehtovaara (eds), *Experiential Learning in Foreign-Language Education* (pp. 8–60). London: Pearson Education.

Kolb, D. (1984). *Experiential Learning: Experience as the Source of Learning and Development* (3rd ed.). Englewood Cliffs, NJ: Prentice Hall.

Kolb, D. (1999). *The Kolb Learning Style Inventory, Version 3.* Boston, MA: Hay Group.

Kooy, M. (2006). The telling stories of novice teachers: Constructing teacher knowledge in book clubs. *Teaching and Teacher Education, 22*, 661–674.

Kramsch, C. (1993). *Context and Culture in Language Teaching.* Oxford: Oxford University Press.

Kramsch, C. (1995). The cultural component of language teaching. *Language, Culture and Curriculum, 8*(2), 83–92.

Kramsch, C. (2011). The symbolic dimensions of the intercultural. *Language Teaching, 44*, 354–367.

Kramsch, C. and Nolden, T. (1994). Redefining literacy in a foreign language. *Die Unterrichtspraxis/Teaching German, 27*(1), 28–35.

Kubanyiova, M. and Feryok, A. (2015). Language teacher cognition in applied linguistics research: Revisiting the territory, redrawing the boundaries, reclaiming the relevance. *The Modern Language Journal, 99*(3), 435–449.

Kubota, R. (2001). Teaching world Englishes to native speakers of English in the USA. *World Englishes, 20*(1), 47–64.

Lambert, W. E (1974). Culture and language as factors in learning and education. In F. E. Aboud and R. D. Meade (eds), *Cultural Factors in Learning and Education.* Bellingham, WA: Western Washington State College.

Langran, I. (2011). Global citizenship, governance, and identity in the post-Westphalian age. Paper presented at the annual meeting of the Northeastern Political Science Association in Philadelphia, PA.

Lanvers, U. (2011). Language Education Policy in England: Is English the elephant in the room? *Apples – Journal of Applied Language Studies, 5*(3), 63–78.

Lanvers, U. (2012). 'The Danish speak so many languages it's really embarrassing'. The impact of L1 English on adult language students' motivation. *Innovation in Language Learning and Teaching, 6*(2), 157–175.

Lanvers, U., Hultgren, K. and Gayton, A. M. (2016). 'People can be smarter with two languages': Changing anglophone students' attitudes to language learning through teaching linguistics. *The Language Learning Journal*, 1–17.

Lawes, S. (2000). The unique contribution of Modern Foreign Languages to the curriculum. In K. Field (ed.), *Issues in Modern Foreign Languages Teaching* (chapter 6). London: Routledge.

Lázár, I. (2015). EFL learners' intercultural competence development in an international web collaboration project. *The Language Learning Journal, 43*(2), 208–221.

Levine, G. S. and Phipps, A. (2012). *Critical and Intercultural Theory and Language Pedagogy.* Boston, MA: Heinle Cengage Learning.

Lewis, G., Jones, B. and Baker, C. (2012). Translanguaging: Developing its conceptualisation and contextualisation. *Educational Research and Evaluation, 18*(7), 655–670.

Liddicoat, A. J. (2005). Culture for language learning in Australian language-in-education policy. *Australian Review of Applied Linguistics, 28*(2), 28–43.

Liddicoat, A. J. (2014). Pragmatics and intercultural mediation in intercultural language learning. *Intercultural Pragmatics, 11*, 259–277.

Liddicoat, A. and Scarino, A. (2010). Eliciting the intercultural in foreign language education at school. In L. Sercu and A. Paran (eds), *Testing the Untestable in Language and Education.* Clevedon, UK: Multilingual Matters.

Liddicoat, A. and Scarino, A. (2013). *Intercultural Language Teaching and Learning.* Chichester: Wiley.

Liddicoat, A. J., Papademetre, L., Scarino, A. and Kohler, M. (2003). Report on Intercultural Language Learning. Canberra: Department of Education, Science and Training.

Lilley, K., Barker, M. and Harris, N. (2017). The global citizen conceptualized: Accommodating ambiguity. *Journal of Studies in International Education, 21*(1), 6–21.

Lister, R. (2003). Investing in the citizen-workers of the future: Transformations on citizenship and the state under New Labour. *Social Policy and Administration, 37*(5), 427–443.

Lo Bianco, J. (2010). Some ideas about multilingualism and national identity. *TESOL in Context, 20*(1), 22.

Lortie, D. (1975). *Schoolteacher: A Sociological Study.* Chicago: University of Chicago Press.

Luke, A. and Luke, C. (2000). A situated perspective on cultural globalisation. In N. Burbules and C. Torres (eds), *Globalization and Education: Critical Perspectives* (pp. 275–297). New York: Routledge.

Lumby, T. (2017). The trouble with citizenship. Downloaded at: https://www.tes.com/news/tes-magazine/tes-magazine/trouble-citizenship

Macaro, E. (2003). *Teaching and Learning a Second Language.* London: Continuum.

McCrone, D. and Bechhofer, F. (2008). National identity and social inclusion. *Ethnic and Racial Studies, 31*(7), 1245–1266.

McCutchen, D., Abbott, R. D., Green, L. B., Beretvas, S. N., Cox, S., Potter, N. S., Quiroga, T. and Gray, A. (2002a). Beginning literacy: Links among teacher knowledge, teacher practice, and student learning. *Journal of Learning Disabilities, 35*, 69–86.

McCutchen, D., Harry, D. R., Cunningham, A. E., Cox, S., Sidman, S. and Covill, A. E. (2002b). Reading teachers' knowledge of children's literature and English phonology. *Annals of Dyslexia, 52*, 207–228.

MacIntyre, P. D. (2002). Motivation, anxiety and emotion in second language acquisition. In P. Robinson (ed.), *Individual Differences and Instructed Language Learning* (pp. 45–68). Amsterdam: John Benjamins.

Markus, H. and Nurius, P. (1986). Possible selves. *American Psychologist, 41*, 954–969.

Marshall, T. H. (1950). *Citizenship and Social Class.* Cambridge: Cambridge University Press.

Martin-Jones, M. (2007). Bilingualism, education and the regulation of access to language resources. In M. Heller (ed.), *Bilingualism: A Social Approach* (pp. 161–182). New York: Palgrave Macmillan.

Meier, G. (2014). Our mother tongue is plurilingualism: A framework of orientations for integrated multilingual curricula. In J. Conteh and G. Meier (eds), *The Multilingual Turn in Languages Education: Opportunities and Challenges* (pp. 132–157). Clevedon, UK: Multilingual Matters.

Meier, G. and Daniels, H. (2013). 'Just not being able to make friends': Social interaction during the year abroad in modern languages degrees. *Research Papers in Education, 28*(2), 212–238.

Mezirow, J. (ed.) (2000). *Learning as Transformation: Critical Perspectives on a Theory in Progress*. San Fransisco, CA: Jossey-Bass.

Ministère Education Nationale (2012). *Les Programmes du Collège*. Downloaded at: www.education.gouv.fr/cid81/les-programmes.html#Languesvivantes (accessed 1 September 2016).

Ministerio de Educación y Ciencia (2007). *Real Decreto 1629/2006*. Downloaded at: http://www.boe.es/boe/dias/2007/01/04/pdfs/A00465-00473.pdf (accessed 1 September 2016).

Minor, J. (2001). Using service-learning as part of an ESL program. *The Internet TESL Journal, 7*(4). Downloaded at: http://iteslj.org/Techniques/Minor-ServiceLearning.html

Moats, L. C. (2000). *Improving the Quality of Teacher Preparation in Early Literacy*. Washington, DC: National Governors Association.

Morrell, F. (1996). *Continent Isolated: A Study of the European Dimension in the National Curriculum in England*. London: Federal Trust.

Naseem, M. A. and Hyslop-Margison, E. (2006). Nussbaum's concept of cosmopolitanism: Practical possibility or academic delusion? *Paideusis, 15*, 51–60.

National Council for Curriculum and Assessment (2016a). *Junior Cycle Programme French and German*. Downloaded at: http://www.curriculumonline.ie/getmedia/21c48e0e-497b-4626-91ca-4c5396497d5b/JCSEC08_French_syllabus.pdf (accessed 17 July 2016).

National Council for Curriculum and Assessment (2016b). *Leaving Certificate French Syllabus*. Downloaded at: http://www.curriculumonline.ie/getmedia/52ac0a4a-562b-410a-83f3-02fa2d666f9e/SCSEC15_French_syllabus_eng.pdf (accessed 17 July 2016).

Nelson, J. and Kerr, D. (2006). *Active Citizenship in INCA Countries: Definitions, Policies, Practices and Outcomes*. International Review of Curriculum and Assessment Frameworks Internet Archive. Downloaded at: https://www.nfer.ac.uk/publications/QAC02/QAC02.pdf (accessed 1 July 2017).

Nespor, J. (1987). The role of beliefs in the practice of teaching. *Journal of Curriculum Studies, 19*(4), 317–28.

Nie, N., Junn, J. and Stehlik-Barry, K. (1996). *Education and Democratic Citizenship in America*. Chicago: University of Chicago Press.

Nieto, S. (2010). *Language, Culture, and Teaching: Critical Perspectives*. New York: Routledge.

Nisbett, R. E. and Ross, L. (1980). *Human Inference: Strategies and Shortcoming of Social Judgment*. Englewood Cliff, NJ: Prentice Hall.

Noels, K., Yashima, T. and Zhang, R. (2011). Language, identity and intercultural communication. In J. Jackson (ed.), *The Routledge Handbook of Language and Intercultural Communication* (pp. 52–66). London: Routledge.

Norton, B. (2000). *Identity and Language Learning: Gender, Ethnicity and Educational Change*. Harlow, UK: Longman/Pearson Education Limited.

Norton, B. (2013). *Identity and Language Learning: Extending the Conversation* (2nd ed.). Clevedon, UK: Multilingual Matters.

Nostrand, H. (1989). Authentic texts and cultural authenticity: An editorial. *Modern Language Journal, 73*(1), 49–52.

The Nuffield Foundation (2000). Languages the Next Generation: The Final Report and Recommendations of the Nuffield Languages Inquiry. Downloaded at: https://www.nuffieldfoundation.org/sites/default/files/languages_finalreport.pdf

Nussbaum, M. (2002). Patriotism and cosmopolitanism. In M. C. Nussbaum and J. Cohen (eds), *For Love of Country?* (pp. 2–17). Boston, MA: Beacon Press.

Oates, C. (2007). Education for citizenship: Languages are the key. *Scottish Languages Review*. ISSN 1756-039X.

Ollikainen, A. (2000). European education, European citizenship? *European Education, 32*(3), 6–21.

Orde, H. (2015). The real threat facing Britain is our own isolationism. *The Guardian*.

Downloaded at: https://www.theguardian.com/commentisfree/2015/nov/21/the-real-threat-facing-britain-is-our-own-isolationism (accessed 12 March 2018).

Osler, A. (1998). European citizenship and study abroad: Student teachers' experiences and identities. *Cambridge Journal of Education, 28*(1), 77–96.

Osler, A. (ed.) (2005). *Teachers, Human Rights and Diversity: Educating Citizens in a Multicultural Society.* Stoke-on-Trent, UK: Trentham Books.

Osler, A. (2016). Teaching for cosmopolitan citizenship. *Educational Leadership, 74*(4), 42–46.

Osler, A. and Starkey, H. (1999). Rights, identities and inclusion: European action programmes as political education. *Oxford Review of Education, 25*(1–2), 199–215.

Osler, A. and Starkey, H. (2003). Learning for cosmopolitan citizenship: Theoretical debates and young peoples' experiences. *Educational Review, 55*(3), 243–254.

Osler, A. and Starkey, H. (2005a). *Changing Citizenship: Democracy and Inclusion in Education.* Maidenhead, UK: Open University Press.

Osler, A. and Starkey, H. (2005b). *Citizenship and Language Learning: International Perspectives.* Stoke-on-Trent, UK: Trentham Books.

Osler, A. and Starkey, H. (2015). Education for cosmopolitan citizenship: A framework for language learning. *Argentinian Journal of Applied Linguistics, 3*(2), 30–39.

Osler, A. and Starkey, H. (2018). Extending the theory and practice of education for cosmopolitan citizenship. *Educational Review, 70*(1), 31–40.

Osler, A. and Vincent, K. (2002). *Citizenship and the Challenge of Global Education.* Stoke-on-Trent, UK: Trentham Books.

Otheguy, R., García, O. and Reid, W. (2015). Clarifying translanguaging and deconstructing named languages: A perspective from linguistics. *Applied Linguistics Review, 6*(3), 281–307.

Paul, R. W. and Elder, L. (2002). *Critical Thinking. Tools for Taking Charge of your Professional and Personal Life.* Upper Saddle River, NJ: Pearson.

Peckenpaugh, K. (2012). Intercultural competence: Meeting the bar and falling short in short-term study abroad. In *Proceedings of the Intercultural Competence Conference,* September, Vol. 2, pp. 143–162.

Perry, L., Stoner, K. R., Stoner, L., Wadsworth, D., Page, R. and Tarrant, M. A. (2016). The importance of global citizenship to higher education: The role of short-term study abroad. *London Review of Education and Science, 1*(19), 342–356.

Phelps, G. (2009). Just knowing how to read isn't enough! Assessing knowledge for teaching reading. *Educational Assessment, Evaluation, and Accountability, 21,* 137–154.

Phelps, G. and Schilling, S. (2004). Developing measures of content knowledge for teachers of reading. *Elementary School Journal, 105,* 31–48.

Phillipson, R. (1992). *Linguistic Imperialism.* Oxford: Oxford University Press.

Pitts, M. J. and Brooks, C. F. (2017). Critical pedagogy, internationalisation, and a third space: Cultural tensions revealed in students' discourse. *Journal of Multilingual and Multicultural Development, 38*(3), 251–267.

Porto, M. (2013). Language and intercultural education: An interview with Michael Byram. *Pedagogies: An International Journal, 8*(2), 143–162.

Porto, M. (2014). Intercultural citizenship education in an EFL on-line project in Argentina. *Language and Intercultural Communication, 14,* 245–261.

Porto, M. and Byram, M. (2015). A curriculum for action in the community and intercultural citizenship in Higher Education. *Language, Culture and Curriculum, 28,* 226–242.

Porto, M. and Yulita, L. (2017). Language and intercultural citizenship education for a culture of peace. In M. Byram, I. Golubeva, H. Han and M. Wagner (eds), *From Principles to Practice in Education for Intercultural Citizenship* (pp. 199–224). Clevedon, UK: Multilingual Matters.

Porto, M., Houghton, S. A. and Byram, M. (2017). Intercultural citizenship in the (foreign) language classroom. *Language Teaching Research, 22*(5), 484–498.

Porto, M., Daryai-Hansen, P., Arcuri, M. A. and Schifler, K. (2017). Green Kidz: Young learners engage in intercultural environmental citizenship in an English language classroom in Argentina and Denmark. In M. Byram, I. Golubeva, H. Han and M. Wagner (eds), *From Principles to Practice in Education for Intercultural Citizenship* (pp. 131–158). Clevedon, UK: Multilingual Matters.

Putnam, R. D. (1995). Tuning in, tuning out: The strange disappearance of social capital in America. *PS: Political Science and Politics, 28*(4), 664–683.

Putnam, R. D. (2000). *Bowling Alone: The Collapse and Revival of American Community.* New York: Simon and Schuster.

Qin, S. L. (2005). *Overview of Civic Education in Foreign Countries* (in Chinese). Zhengzhou: Zhengzhou University Press.

Qin, S. L. (2014). A review and vision of civic education in contemporary China. In K. J. Kennedy, G. P. Fairbrother and Z. Zhenxhou (eds), *Citizenship Education in China: Preparing Citizens for the 'Chinese Century'* (pp. 40–66). Abingdon: Routledge.

Qin, S. L., Du, J. and Chen, S. (eds) (2009). *Civics in Foreign Countries* (in Chinese). Zhengzhou: Zhengzhou University Press.

Qualifications and Curriculum Authority (QCA) (1999). *The National Curriculum: Handbook for Primary Teachers in England (Key Stages 1 and 2).* London: HMSO.

Qualifications and Curriculum Authority (QCA) (2007). *Modern Foreign Languages: Programme of Study for Key Stage 3 and Attainment Targets.* Downloaded at: https://webarchive.nationalarchives.gov.uk/20110203184640/http://curriculum.qcda.gov.uk/uploads/QCA-07-3340-p_MFL_KS3_tcm8-405.pdf

Ramirez, E. (2016). Impact on intercultural competence when studying abroad and the moderating role of personality. *Journal of Teaching in International Business, 27*(2–3), 88–105.

Rauschert, P. (2014). *Intercultural Service Learning im Englischunterricht. Ein Modell zur Förderung interkultureller Kompetenz auf der Basis journalistischen Schreibens* [*Intercultural Service Learning in English Language Teaching: A Model to Foster Intercultural Competence on the Basis of Journalistic Writing*]. Münster: Waxmann.

Rauschert, P. and Byram, M. (2018). Service learning and intercultural citizenship in foreign-language education. *Cambridge Journal of Education, 48*(3), 353–369.

Rhoads, R. and Szelenyi, K. (2011). *Global Citizenship and the University: Advancing Social Life and Relations in an Interdependent World.* Stanford, CA: Stanford University Press.

Richards, J. C. (2008). Second language teacher education today. *RELC Journal, 39*(2), 158–177.

Risager, K. (2006). *Language and Culture. Global Flows and Local Complexity.* Clevedon, UK: Multilingual Matters.

Risager, K. (2007). *Language and Culture Pedagogy. From a National to a Transnational Paradigm.* Clevedon, UK: Multilingual Matters.

Rocheleau, J. (2004). Theoretical roots of service-learning: Progressive education and the development of citizenship. In B. W. Speck and S. I. Hoppe (eds), *Service-learning: History, Theory and Issues* (pp. 3–22). Westport, CT: Praeger.

Rojek, C. (2008). *Brit-Myth.* Londong and Chicago: Reaktion.

Ruffer, G. B. (2012). Citizenship. In H. K. Anheier and M. Juergensmeyer (eds), *Encyclopedia of Global Studies.* Thousand Oaks, CA: Sage.

Rydenvald, M. (2015). Elite bilingualism? Language use among multilingual teenagers of Swedish background in European Schools and international schools in Europe. *Journal of Research in International Education, 14*(3), 213–227.

Saville-Troike, M. (2003). *The Ethnography of Communication* (Vol. 3). Oxford: Blackwell.

Scarino, A. and Liddicoat, A.J. (2009). *Teaching and Learning Languages. A Guide.* Melbourne: Melbourne Curriculum Corporation of Australia.

Schartner, A. (2016). The effect of study abroad on intercultural competence: A longitudinal case study of international postgraduate students at a British university. *Journal of Multilingual and Multicultural Development, 37*(4), 402–418.

Schattle, H. (2008). *The Practices of Global Citizenship*. Plymouth, UK: Rowman & Littlefield.

Schulz, W., Ainley, J., Fraillon, J., Losito, B., Agrusti, G. and Friedman, T. (2016). *Becoming Citizens in a Changing World: IEA International Civic and Citizenship Education Study, 2016 International Report*. New York: Springer International Publishing.

Seidlhofer, B. (1996). 'It is an undulating feeling . . .': The importance of being a non-native teacher of English. *VIEWS (Vienna English Working Papers), 5*, 63–79.

Seifert, A. and Zentner, S. (2010). *Service-learning – Lernen durch Engagement: Methode Qualität, Beispiele und ausgewählte Scherpunkte. Eine Publikation des Netzwerks Lernen durch Engagement*. Weinheim: Freudenberg Stiftung.

Sercu, L. (2006). The foreign language and intercultural competence teacher: The acquisition of a new professional identity. *Intercultural Education, 17*(1), 55–72.

Sercu, L., with Bandura, E., Castro, P., Davcheva, L., Laskaridou, C., Lundgren, U., Mendez García, M. and Ryan, P. (2005). *Foreign Language Teachers and Intercultural Communication: An International Investigation*. Clevedon, UK: Multilingual Matters.

Shariatmadari, D. (2016). I'm being stripped of my citizenship – along with 65 million others. Downloaded at: https://www.theguardian.com/commentisfree/2016/oct/07/eu-citizenship-stripped-brexit-theresa-may

Shukra, K., Back, L., Keith, M., Khan, A. and Solomos, J. (2004). Race, social cohesion and the changing politics of citizenship. *London Review of Education, 2*(3), 187–195.

Sigauke, A. T. (2012). Young people, citizenship and citizenship education in Zimbabwe. *International Journal of Educational Development, 32*(2), 214–223.

Skinner, Q. (1986). The paradoxes of political liberty. In S. M. McMurrin (ed.), *Tanner Lectures on Human Values, VII*. Salt Lake City: University of Utah Press.

Sliwka, A. and Frank, S. (2004). *Service Learning. Verantwortung lernen in Schule und Gemeinde* [*Service Learning. Education towards Responsibility in Schools and in the Community*]. Weinheim/Basel: Beltz Verlag.

Snow, M. A. (2001). Content-based and immersion models for second and foreign language teaching. *Teaching English as a Second or Foreign Language, 3*, 303–318.

Speck, B. W. and Hoppe, S. L. (2004). *Service-learning: History, Theory and Issues*. Westport, CT: Praeger.

Spitzberg, B. H. and Changnon, G. (2009). Conceptualising intercultural competence. In D. Deardorff (ed.), *The Sage Handbook of Intercultural Competence* (pp. 2–52). Los Angeles: Sage.

Staeheli, L. (1999). Globalization and the scales of citizenship. *Geography Research Forum*, 19, 60–77.

Starkey, H. (2002). Language teaching, citizenship, human rights and intercultural education. In A. Swarbrick (ed.), *Teaching Modern Foreign Languages in Secondary Schools: A Reader* (pp. 95–111). London: Routledge.

Starkey, H. (2005). Language teaching for democratic citizenship. In A. Osler and H. Starkey (eds), *Citizenship and Language Learning: International Perspectives* (pp. 23–41). Stoke-on-Trent, UK: Trentham Books.

Stewart, A. (1995). Two conceptions of citizenship. *British Journal of Sociology, 46*(1), 63–78.

Stewart, A. (2000). Never ending story: Inclusion and exclusion in late modernity. In P. Askonas and A. Stewart (eds), *Social Inclusion: Possibilities and Tensions* (pp. 55–72). London: Macmillan.

Sulleyman, A. (2017). Brexit leads to surge in Brits wanting to learn new language, data finds. Downloaded at: http://www.independent.co.uk/life-style/gadgets-and-tech/news/brexit-uk-foreign-language-surge-french-spanish-german-lingvist-a7724831.html

Sung, C. C. M. (2016). ESL university students' perceptions of their global identities in

English as a lingua franca communication: A case study at an international university in Hong Kong. *The Asia-Pacific Education Researcher*, *25*(2), 305–314.

Sutherland, L., Howard, S. and Markauskaite, L. (2010). Professional identity creation: Examining the development of beginning preservice teachers' understanding of their work as teachers. *Teaching and Teacher Education*, *26*, 455–465.

Taylor, W. H. (1993). Educating British children for European citizenship *European Journal of Education*, *28*(4), 437–444.

Tonge, J., Mycock, A. and Jeffery, B. (2012). Does citizenship education make young people better-engaged citizens? *Political Studies*, *60*(3), 578–602.

Trejo, P. (2010). Developing generic cultural awareness through collaborative wiki- facilitated projects. Unpublished MA dissertation, The University of Manchester.

Trejo, P. and Fay, R. (2013). Developing general cultural awareness in a moncultural English as a foreign language context in a Mexican university: A wiki-based critical incident approach. *Language Learning Journal*, *43*(2), 222–233.

United Nations High Commissioner for Refugees (UNHCF) (2018). *Global Trends: Forced Displacement in 2017*. Downloaded at: https://www.unhcr.org/5b27be547.pdf

United States Congress (1990). *National and Community Service Act*. Downloaded at: https://www.uscg.mil/Portals/0/Headquarters/civilrights/PDFs/history/ncsa1990.pdf

Valdés, G. and Figueroa, R. (1994). *Bilingualism and Testing: A Special Case of Bias*. Norwood, NJ: Ablex Publishing Corporation.

van Ek, J. (1986). *Objectives for Foreign Language Learning. Vol. 1: Scope*. Strasbourg: Council of Europe.

Vandrick, S. (1995). Privileged ESL university students. *TESOL Quarterly*, *29*(2), 375–381.

Varghese, M., Morgan, B., Johnston, B. and Johnson, K. A. (2005). Theorizing language teacher identity: Three perspectives and beyond. *Journal of Language, Identity, and Education*, *4*, 21–44.

Vaughan, E. (2007). 'I think we should just accept . . . our horrible lowly status': Analysing teacher–teacher talk within the context of community of practice. *Language Awareness*, *16*(3), 173–189.

Verba, S., Schlozman, K. L. and Brady, H. E. (1995) *Voice and Equality: Civic Voluntarism in American Politics*. Cambridge, MA: Harvard University Press.

Vermeulen, J. (2004). Citizenship and linguistic inequality. In R. Maier (ed.), *Citizenship and Identity* (pp. 141–160). Maastricht: Shaker Publications.

Wagner, M., Conlon Perugini, D. and Byram, M. (eds) (2017). *Teaching Intercultural Competence Across the Age Range: From Theory to Practice*. Clevedon, UK: Multilingual Matters.

Walkington, H. and Wilkins, C. (2000). Education for critical citizenship: The impact of teachers' world view on classroom practice in the teaching of values. *The School Field*, *11*(1/2), 59–78.

Wang, X. W. (ed.) (2003). *Comparative Moral Education* (in Chinese). Wuhan: Wuhan University Press.

Warford, M. K. (2011). The zone of proximal teacher development. *Teaching and Teacher Education*, *27*(2), 252–258.

Weedon, C. (1997). *Feminist Practice and Poststructuralist Theory* (2nd ed.). London: Blackwell.

Wenger, E. (1998). Communities of practice: Learning as a social system. *Systems Thinker*, *9*(5), 2–3.

Wenger, E. (2008). Communities of practice: A new discipline of learning. Unpublished seminar paper.

Whiteley, P. (2005) Citizenship Education Longitudinal Study: Second Literature Review. Citizenship Education: The Political Science Perspective National Foundation for Educational Research: University of Essex.

Wiener, A. (1996). Making sense of the new geography of citizenship: Fragmented citizenship in the European Union. Paper presented at the European University Institute, Florence, Italy, 22–4 February 1996.

Williams, M. and Burden, R. (1997). *Psychology for Language Teachers*. Cambridge: Cambridge University Press.

Willingham, D. (2007). Critical thinking: Why is it so hard to teach? *American Educator*, *31*(2), 8–19.

Wong Fillmore, L. and Snow, C. (2002). What teachers need to know about language. In C. A. Adger, C. E. Snow and D. Christian (eds), *What Teachers Need to Know About Language* (pp. 7–54). McHenry, IL: Delta Systems; Washington, DC: Center for Applied Linguistics.

Wright, T. (1992). L2 classroom research and L2 teacher education: Towards a collaborative approach. In J. Flowerdew, M. Brock and S. Hsia (eds), *Perspectives on Second Language Teacher Education* (pp. 187–209). Hong Kong: City Polytechnic of Hong Kong.

Wright, T. (2010). Second language teacher education: Review of recent research on practice. *Language Teaching*, *43*(3), 259–296.

Wringe, C. (1999). Issues in education for citizenship at national, local and global levels. *The Development Education Journal*, *6*(1), 4–6.

Young, T. J. and Schartner, A. (2014). The effects of cross-cultural communication education on international students' adjustment and adaptation. *Journal of Multilingual and Multicultural Development*, *35*(6), 547–562.

Youth Service America (YSA) (2007). *Addressing Diversity and Global Challenges through Intercultural Service Learning*. Washington, DC: YSA. Downloaded at: http://tools.ysa.org/downloads/modules/InterculturalService-LearningModule.pdf

Yuan, R. and Lee, I. (2015). The cognitive, social and emotional processes of teacher identity construction in a pre-service teacher education programme. *Research Papers in Education*, *30*(4), 469–491.

# Index

Printed and bound by PG in the USA